complicated questions that are gnawing at the souls of women, both Christian and secular.

The responses God gives, though not always easy to digest, provide a deeper understanding of eternal truth than might have been expected. These straightforward answers are precise and concise and, best of all, biblically based. What else would the reader expect from one who loves the Lord and cares deeply for women's issues like Julie."

—**Joe Ragont**, Bible teacher; author of *40 Days to Your Best Life for Prime-Timers*

THE
GOD
INTERVIEWS

Questions You Would Ask;
Answers God Gives

Julie-Allyson Ieron

LEAFWOOD
PUBLISHERS

THE GOD INTERVIEWS

Questions You Would Ask; Answers God Gives

Copyright 2012 by Julie-Allyson Ieron

ISBN 978-0-89112-352-1

LCCN 2012016172

Printed in the United States of America

LIBRARY OF CONGRESS CATALOGING-IN-PUBLICATION DATA

Ieron, Julie-Allyson.
  The God interviews : questions you would ask, answers God gives / Julie-Allyson Ieron.
    p. cm.
  ISBN 978-0-89112-352-1
  1. Christian women--Religious life--Miscellanea. 2. God (Christianity)--Miscellanea. I. Title.
  BV4527.I37 2012
  248.8'43--dc23

                                                                          2012016172

Cover design by Greg Golden
Interior text design by Sandy Armstrong

Leafwood Publishers is an imprint of
Abilene Christian University Press
1626 Campus Court
Abilene, Texas 79601

1-877-816-4455
www.leafwoodpublishers.com

12 13 14 15 16 17 / 7 6 5 4 3 2 1

To all my Bible teachers down through the years—
especially Mom, Dad, and Papa Tony—
who modeled for me the way to dig into God's Word,
meet Him there, and discover for myself His answers
to the greatest questions of all.

Thanks To:

Greg Johnson and Rachelle Gardner at WordServe Literary for believing in the creative concept of this book and persisting in finding it a home.

The Leafwood team and especially Gary Myers for his vision in choosing the project and working with me to craft a killer title, Robyn Burwell for her insightful editorial shepherding, Leonard Allen for his vision for the cover, and the marketing crew for getting this book into your hands.

Contents

Invitation to
The GOD Interviews

Are women supposed to have midlife crises? I mean *really*. Isn't that particular curse supposed to be the domain of the guys? Or is this another of the downsides of pursuing equality—ranking right up there with the rising rates of women suffering from heart attacks?

I don't know the answer to the "supposed to" part of the midlife crisis question, but I do know this—when I hit forty, the big questions of life hit me with a vengeance. I suppose forty is that magic number where (male and female alike) we can no longer deny the fact that we've hit something close to the middle point of life. It stands to reason we'd take some time to analyze just how valuable our efforts have been to this point.

I don't know many people who are satisfied with their current life stage. We all dream of having something we don't have, and, at life's midpoint, we start to imagine we might never achieve all our best dreams. I was definitely *there*.

And, as it happened, around that time the entire planet entered a crisis of its own—a global economic earthquake. As an entrepreneur of more than ten years, I suddenly found myself watching client after client eliminate employees, merge, go bankrupt, close, or otherwise dry up. No matter your industry, you watched the same thing happen to people in your world—it may even have happened to you.

Like the disciple Peter and his fishing buddies, James and John, in the hours after they watched their Master crucified, I was ready to give up and return to my nets—or, in my case, to in-office publishing work on a regular payroll. Except, traditional publishing was in danger of becoming a dinosaur in the new economy, too.

So I floundered.

Call it midlife crisis. Call it redirection. Call it a course correction that was a long time coming. All I know is that with an intensity I'd never before experienced, I found myself re-evaluating absolutely everything. I had reached that moment when unanswerable questions were just about bowling me over:

- Why am I here?
- Is there some task I've been assigned?
- Have I measured up to the unseen standard, or am I falling short?
- Am I charging windmills, or is there still something to conquer on my current life path?
- Do I need to regroup, retool, and redirect?
- Is there some plan I'm supposed to find? If there is, I don't even know where to begin looking for it.

If we were to chat, you and I, you'd probably admit to harboring a similar list of questions you'd like to ask about your place in this world. I suppose if we live long enough, all of us will come up against life-altering questions that nag for resolution.

An expert. That's what I needed to find. Someone who would offer context and wisdom.

One of my favorite aspects of being a full-time writer/journalist (the career I was *this close* to chucking) is the opportunity to conduct interviews with experts on any subject you can name. The challenge is to find the right expert, ask the right questions, and sift through the answers to find gems that will make a difference in real life.

I've also spent a considerable amount of time sitting on the flip side of the interview table—being considered an "expert" on topics ranging from time management (from my book *Conquering the Time Factor*), to workplace integrity (from *Staying True in a World of Lies*), to caring for the aging (from *The Overwhelmed Woman's Guide to . . . Caring for Aging Parents*), to how to be a professional writer (from my many years of *being* one).

As a recognized expert, I have a good perspective on just how *un*expert we experts really are. Sure, we've done research or lived through a subject, but our perspective is painfully limited.

All that to say, as I looked for a qualified expert to answer the questions that might preside over the second half of my life (should I have another four decades on the planet) I could think of only one who truly fit the bill. So, as a trained journalist who happens to be a believer in God and a follower of His Son Jesus Christ, I conjured up in my mind a scenario where I'd take my stockpile of insistent questions to the supreme source of wisdom in the universe and see what He has to say to them. That's why I issued an invitation to the ultimate Guest to join me on the imaginary set of *The GOD Interviews*.

I suppose my approach wasn't altogether different from that of the ancient seeker, Job, who watched his world crumble, grieved over the misguided counsel of his friends and his wife, and finally found an audience in the throne room of Almighty God.

But I'm not Job. I'm a twenty-first-century woman. A seeker after God? Desiring a wisdom beyond my own? Desperate for a pattern to build my life upon? Yes, yes, and yes.

So, then, would God come join me on the interview set? Would He offer viable answers to my heartfelt questions? Would His answers, if He offered them, be relevant to women everywhere?

Read on and find out. Because if there's one thing I'm certain about as I begin this interview of interviews: it will yield unexpected answers to life's most compelling questions. It won't be glib or easy or quick, but it will be rich and challenging and ultimately, fulfilling.

So, now, turn on your view screen, crank up the volume, and listen in on my interview of a lifetime, my GOD Interview.

— Chapter 1 —

What Do You Want from Me?

Scene: Soundstage. *Most of the room is strewn with cameras, half-wound cables, high-intensity lights, and disassembled microphones. Within view of three cameras sits a made-for-TV faux office scene featuring a conference table and set with two chairs opposite each other.*

A forty-something woman in a business suit is in one chair. She shuffles through notes, reading and rereading, alternately taking a swig from a sweaty water bottle and checking her watch. Her leg bounces to an inaudible beat.

A Producer, Floor Director, Camera Operator, and a full contingent of production crew wait to record the interaction, should it take place. They nibble on snacks and kibitz about current events, family gossip, and plans for the weekend.

And then . . . the room freezes in time as an awesome Presence steps onto the set. Unworldly bodyguards with flashing bodies and gleaming swords open a wide path for Him to take the seat across from the woman.

The crew moves as if by rote. The Floor Director hands a lavaliere micro-phone to one of the bodyguards, who weaves it through the Guest's gar-ments. The Producer gives a signal to begin recording. Without so much as a "lights, camera, action," the GOD Interview begins. The Guest's voice, strangely calm yet unbendingly firm, addresses the Reporter:

You asked to speak with Me.

Yyyy. That is to say—yes, Ssssss-ir. Yes I did. But now . . .

Here I am. Ask Me anything.

Really? Anything?

Yes.

Okay. Well, I, uh, suddenly can't seem to read my notes.

You know, there is no need to be afraid.

Actually, I now realize there is. My clothes are a little soiled and pretty wrinkled . . . I'm not exactly perfectly prepared for this. Maybe this is a really bad idea. No, I'm *sure* it is. I'm really sorry I bothered You . . .

It is no bother.

He holds out a hand, hollowed out and scarred at the wrist, and stops the woman from leaving the table.

I am glad you asked to see Me.

You are?

Sure. I am not intimidated by questions, and, quite honestly, there are no questions the mind I have given you could come up with that would shock Me or stump Me. Ask Me anything. I saw your list, and I would very much like to answer. Which of the questions is most pressing on your heart? I want to answer you first. Then, I will address the questions from your viewers.

Wow. My question? Okay . . . where to begin? Maybe I should give you some context.

If you would like; although, it is not strictly necessary.

Well, I'm just over forty . . .

I know.

Yes, well, I suppose You would. So you know my life's gotten pretty depressing. I don't like where I am—in fact, I'm not even sure I like who I am. I've never worked harder in my life or put in more pound-the-pavement hours, but my bank account is plunging to frightening levels. To top it off, I'm awfully lonely, and to make matters worse, I'm not pleasant to be around. I'm feeling useless—like You've put me on a shelf and moved on to another place without me.

Hmmm.

Well, that's why I want to talk to You. I've tried for years to do what I think would make You happy, but I'm wondering if I've succeeded at anything. Am I on the wrong track? Is that why I'm feeling so blah, so used up and valueless? What do You want from me? Tell me, and I'll try to measure up. But it's hard to measure up to a standard I can't see. What do You want from me?

At church yesterday morning, I was at once shocked and heartened when our guest preacher (Associate Pastor Greg Norwine, who is about my age) validated Reporter's (and my) issue. He, a solid, self-assured pastor, admitted that he recently went through a season of asking God, at this middle point, for confirmation and direction—a type of job performance review. He wanted to be sure he doesn't get too far down a road before being certain it's one God would have him follow.

Pastor Greg's answer came from words penned by a post-midlife apostle Paul, who had done a big self-evaluation as he sat imprisoned and facing a death sentence. Paul wrote, "For to me to live is Christ . . ." (Phil.

1:21). The pastor's definition of this kind of living was twofold: "The life filled with unsinkable joy is at once spent in exalting and serving Christ," he said.

Nice words. They have a ring of truth to them because an ancient saint lived them out with great success. But are they a little out of touch for a woman of today? Could they possibly be of real use to us in our overwhelmed days that stretch on far into the night hours?

I wonder what answer Christ would give to the question of what He wants from each of us as His individual children. Since our interview scene is only fiction (like you hadn't figured that out), I needed to find an answer that would work in the world of nonfiction—the world where we live. So, I did the only thing available to a modern woman and the next best thing to a live interview—I combed through the words God spoke about Himself and the direction He gave to His people about what He expected of them. And, wouldn't you know it, I found a pointed and specific answer to our precise question.

Now, it'll take some unpacking to see how it applies to real life, but it's right there spelled out in black and white—or on tablets or on scrolls or however it was originally recorded several millennia ago by the prophet Micah.

God, what do You want from us?, the people asked. *Do You want sacrifice? Do You want homage? Do You want the people and things most precious to us? What do You want from us?* That's exactly what God's people were asking Him in Micah 6:6–7:

> You say, "What can I bring with me
> when I come before the Lord,
> when I bow before God on high?
> Should I come before him with burnt offerings,
> with year-old calves?
> Will the Lord be pleased with a thousand male sheep?
> Will he be pleased with ten thousand rivers of oil?

> Should I give my first child for the evil I have done?
> Should I give my very own child for my sin?" (NCV)

With each question, the obvious, if unspoken, answer from the Almighty Lord was, *No, of course that's not what I want*. And then, since they just didn't get it (don't quibble, we don't often get it either), here's what He said, plain and simple in the next verse:

> The LORD has told you, human, what is good;
> he has told you what he wants from you:
> to do what is right to other people,
> love being kind to others,
> and live humbly, obeying your God. (Mic. 6:8 NCV)

To put it the way I memorized it in Sunday school decades ago, the Lord requires of us these three simple things: to act justly, to love mercy, and to walk humbly with your God.

If that's what He required of His people in Old Testament times, did His expectations change under the new agreement put in place when Jesus died and rose again? I don't think so. Because when Jesus was talking to both scoffers and followers in Matthew 9:13, He echoed the Micah passage with this directive: "I desire mercy, and not sacrifice." In Mark 12:33 He added, "To love [the Lord] with all . . . [your] strength, and to love one's neighbor as yourself, is much more than all whole burnt offerings and sacrifices." He supplemented that with a grave indictment of the religious leaders of His day, "Woe to you. . . . [You] neglect justice and the love of God" (Luke 11:42).

Clearly, His expectations haven't changed: justice, mercy, and knowing our place before Creator God—clear and concise. But are they as simple as they appear at first glance, and how do they impact life as we know it? To uncover the truth about what this trilogy of requirements means in real time, let's address each phrase individually.

To Act Justly

I love the line in the imaginary interview where the Reporter says, "I've tried for years to do what I think would make You happy." In essence she's saying, along with many of us, *I've tried to do the right thing at every opportunity. True, I haven't always succeeded, but I've tried. Does that count for anything?*

We all have that innate sense of right and wrong. We all have a tendency to do wrong that, truth be told, offends even our own sense of behaving justly. I suspect this innate sense of right and wrong is placed there by our Creator, the one Who establishes the measure of justice for the universe. According to *Easton's Bible Dictionary,* "Justice is not an optional product of [God's] will, but an unchangeable principle of his very nature."[1]

God's justice makes me happy in one sense. He can be trusted to accurately weigh and measure the actions of others and hold them accountable to an exacting standard. I want *honorable* and *fair* to be the watchwords of others' dealings with me—in business practices, in relationships, in matters of medicine and law, and in everyday life.

Surely you'll agree that those who serve the greater good in our society need to be honorable. Not long ago when the economic dominoes began to tumble as the American banking industry was called to account for bad loans, mismanagement, or simply poor business decisions, the blame game started. The Republicans blamed the Democratic-controlled Congress. The Democrats blamed the Republican in the White House. Instead of searching for a just solution, they searched for scapegoats. As for me (one of those lumped into the "voting public" category who have little control over unfolding events like these), I just wanted to blame 'em all and throw 'em out of office come November.

That's just about the absolute antithesis of what God's expectations of acting justly would call for. Bible commentary writer Michael J. Wilkins explains this way: "It is right to want to see justice prevail. But it is wrong when my ego gets in the way—when I retaliate to prove that I am strong, that I am superior to the other person, that I am the almighty righteous cop for God."[2]

Yes, I'm quick to call for just behavior on someone else's part—and in some cases, it might even be my right to do so. But that's not what God's holy requirement through the prophet Micah is concerned about. He tells *me* to "act justly." This is not a place where He calls me to hold *someone else* to a just standard. Rather, the requirement is to do justice myself.

I've already admitted to you that I've fallen far short of the exacting standard of a just God. No matter the details of how, how often, or when I've repented and tried to salvage my own messed-up situations, the bottom line is I simply don't measure up, anymore than our reporter friend does. I know it. She knows it. You know it about yourself. God knows it about all of us.

So, this whole matter of behaving justly is a little harder than it seems. That's where the second part of the command comes to my rescue. I think you'll be as glad as I am that God's expectations for us didn't stop with acting justly.

To Love Mercy

I love mercy. I'm sure you do, too. Especially when it's directed toward each of us. When I don't measure up. When I miss God's mark. When I sin and can't help but come face to face with the fact that, as far as the perfection standard, "my clothes are a little soiled and pretty wrinkled," as the Reporter rightly notes about herself. It's then I'm grateful for mercy—the unmerited kindness of God. It's the heartbeat of the dying Christ on the cross who cries out, "Father, forgive them, because they do not know what they are doing" (Luke 23:34 HCSB).

That kind of mercy is easy to love. The one that cuts me slack and gives me a way out of a debt I could never begin to repay. Yeah, God! I can do this. I can measure up to this standard of Yours—I *do* love mercy.

Or do I? Do I find mercy as easy to dish out as it is to take in? Because I'm pretty sure, on a second read of the command, that it's a two-way street.

Consider several friends I've known (you probably know someone who's lived through a similar experience) each of whom was confronted at midlife by a husband of twenty-plus years who decided he no longer wanted to be married to her; in fact, he wasn't sure he'd ever really loved her at all.

How hard is mercy to offer then? Wouldn't she really rather exact justice on him—or at least take him legally for everything she can and make his life as miserable as possible for the foreseeable future? Isn't it her right to make him justly pay for the pain he caused and all his selfishness stole from her?

Or consider someone I know whose father died in the hospital during what was supposed to be a routine procedure, and there existed the real possibility that an error by the medical team was to blame for his death. Is that man's family able to offer mercy? Wouldn't justice be sweet? Wouldn't it be just to drag those doctors to court and exact damages due to their negligence? What jury of the family's peers would deny them justice?

What good is justice to these friends? Will it stop a husband from leaving, put twenty years of love back into a marriage, or bring back a loved one? Then again, would mercy do much better for them?

I think a look at the choice not to offer mercy may help. Years after the fact, the bitterness of *un*forgiveness won't be causing any pain to the offenders. They could have gone on and lived happy, productive lives oblivious to the hurt they've caused. The *un*forgiven may not even sense the lack of mercy. But our unforgiving friends will be bitter and angry and stunted in their growth. For the lack of being able to love mercy, they will have wasted their lives—always rehearsing and even relishing the events in their minds, keeping their anger fueled and their hurt fresh. Who has really suffered?

Even the definition of mercy is wrapped up in the concept of unmerited, un-asked-for pardon. Where justice is properly due or merited, mercy is its flipside. Interesting that God's simple trilogy of requirements would include these opposites—justice and mercy. How could this be?

In the options that stand before these people, I'm beginning to see the inadequacy of acting justly alone. To act justly can be but one portion of God's answer to the question of what He wants from each of us. Without the balancing act of mercy, justice exacted would be a bitter pill.

I saw mercy in operation in a sitcom rerun the other night (no, I don't sleep nights, do you?). It was an *All in the Family* episode where Archie had cheated on Edith, and she was deciding whether to forgive him. She didn't seem inclined to do so, so Archie asked how long she intended to hold it against him—for the rest of his life?

She thought for a long moment. You could see justice and mercy fighting for supremacy. She had every right to hold it against him, and the actress had us all believing that was what she was going to do. But then she answered, "No," with a catch in her throat and a face disfigured with pain, "Because that would be the rest of *my* life, too." Wisdom from the mouth of a simple character.

So we work at acting justly while loving mercy—mercy toward others and mercy offered to us. Together these two elements of the trilogy will keep us clear of potential handicaps that would hinder us from moving forward in God's purposes for our lives.

But there's still more. Read on.

To Walk Humbly With God

I suppose humility before God is the rational response to the picture we've already painted. Trying to act justly but knowing so well our own failure. Loving the mercy offered to us at great cost to God's Son, so we wouldn't get what we justly deserve—and then taking it to the next level by offering the same measure of mercy toward those who have wronged us. Taken together, it's easy to see that the heart having once received mercy from God would have a proper perspective of her own standing in His sight.

What does this look like in real time? I think in this case, the Reporter got it right. When she was confronted face to face with God, her attitude changed. Her self-assurance, her journalistic pride in the people's right to know, her last vestige of smugness abandoned her. In His presence, she saw herself as wrinkled and sullied from brushes with the world. She backed away, feeling unprepared and unworthy of an audience with Him.

It is at that point that the Master stepped in and drew her back to the table to carry on a heartfelt conversation with Him. And it is at the point of our realizing our great need for Him, our deserving of justice, our desperation for mercy, that He meets us as well. Only in our humility are we primed to open ourselves to Him—heart and soul. Only then are we willing to listen to Him and conform to what we hear Him ask of us.

We'll have many more questions, and we'll even revisit this question later to examine it from another perspective, but we've made a start now. Let's see what else He has to say to us.

And Now, Back to Our Interview . . .

Since you asked, let me tell you, modern woman, what is good and what I want from you. I want you to act justly; I want you to love showing mercy; I want you to have a proper understanding of the treasure house of mercy I've offered to you.

I'm beginning to get it. At least I think I am.

Would it help to put it in your own words—just to be sure?

Actually, that might be good. What I'm hearing You say is You want me to have an accurate picture of who I am and to be concerned with the plight of others—those who are stepped on, feeling down, and even those who have wronged me and deserve justice. And then you want me to look to You to learn how to apply these instructions to my choices, my actions, and my attitudes today.

You have it. Now, I know there is more you want to know, so ask on, My friend.

Discussion Questions

1. Justice is one of the key requirements God has for us. Using Psalm 37:28 as your example, paint a word picture of your definition of justice. Describe the difference between expecting others to measure up to that definition and holding yourself to that standard.

2. The Reporter, who found herself face to face with the Living Christ, caught a glimpse of herself standing before Him. Read Isaiah 53:6 to learn what God did to establish you in right standing before Him. Write about your response to this gift of mercy.

3. The wise Solomon wrote that humility's reward is great. Check out what he said in Proverbs 22:4. How does this line up with your experience? How does this help you see why God makes a big deal about knowing our place before Him?

Author's Note

Each chapter will conclude with questions like these. They're crafted to get you thinking about how Christ would interact with you in each of the true-to-life situations you encounter while reading this book. You might want to get out your Bible and your journal to chronicle your thoughts. Better yet, why not gather some trusted friends and fellow readers to hash these out together?

Chapter 2

Why Did You Make Me the Way I Am?

The disembodied voice of the Producer calls the stage to attention from the control room.

Okay, team. Look alive! Oh, Sir, I didn't mean You. I mean, I didn't mean to imply . . . I just meant . . .

You did not offend Me. I *am* alive, after all.

Yes, well . . . I need the crew to people their stations; our first live linkup is ready. Sir, are You ready for a tough one?

I always do My best.

The Guest turns toward the Reporter, who is sitting taller across from Him as she addresses the Producer.

Hey, P. Who's queued up first?

Disgruntled in Delaware.

Hmm. DD. Let me find her in my notes. Oh, yes, she is a challenge—maybe not the best one to start us out? Sir, this one may not be very respectful, but she's had it really rough. Can you cut her some slack?

I have done better than that for her already.

Sure. Okay. You'll look right at that bigger screen up top and see Disgruntled. She has a monitor and can see and hear what goes on in the studio. In case You're wondering how You look to her, there's the monitor for Your camera down below.

Efficient set-up. Nice use of technology.

Thanks.

The Producer breaks in from the control room as the monitor screens light up with test patterns.

We'll cut live to DD in four . . . three . . .

As the Stage Director counts down two and one, Disgruntled's face appears. She locks angry eyes on the Guest. The Reporter tries to soften the embarrassment of such a brazen challenge.

Go ahead, there in Delaware. You're face to face with our Honored Guest.

Oh, yeah! I'm here—and it's about time.

Hello there, Disgruntled. It is good to see you. Now, you and I both know *Disgruntled* is not the name you were meant to have. But, I will honor your wishes and call you by that name for now.

He is disarming, isn't He DD?

Is He ready to listen to me, or not?

I am listening.

Look here. Camera Operator, pan out a little, so He can see the whole scene. See this chair, this *wheel*chair? I'm thirty-three years old, and this is where I'm stuck. And You—You made me this way. In fact, You did a pretty crummy job on this model right from the start.

Thirty-three? My own thirty-third year was exceptionally painful—so I do feel your pain.

Humph. You have no idea!

The Producer signals for the main screen to cut to a photo montage from DD's early years. It shows scraped knees from losing her balance on the playground, her complexion as pale as the hospital sheets surrounding her as she spent her eleventh Christmas in Children's Memorial, and fiery red-faced as she received a hopeless, end-of-the-road diagnosis from the world's leading specialist on her degenerative disease when she was in her teens.

See all that? That's my life. From bad to worse. Now to *this!* Why did You bother making me at all if You were going to sentence me to bondage in this defective, useless bag of bones?

You know, Honored Guest, DD's situation is pretty extreme, but I know I've been through many days when I've felt her kind of emotion. I don't always like who I am—who You made me to be. I don't think she and I are alone here. Would You respond to this question for women everywhere: Why didn't You make me some other way? Why am I the way I am?

Forgive me for leaving you (and Disgruntled) hanging in midair by interrupting the conversation before our Lord has the opportunity to answer. I've found that often we internalize truths so much better when we discover answers through our own intent searching rather than allowing someone to do a data dump on us. So, I'd like us to work together here, to both examine Disgruntled's question and discover some of what God might say to her.

Of course, none of *us* would be so presumptuous as to ask such a blatantly loaded question of God—or would we?

Behind the Question

It may be as pesky as wondering why He gave us fuzzy brown hair when we really wanted feathery blonde tresses, or why our skin blemishes didn't clear up when we cleared puberty. It may be as frustrating as wondering why He chose to saddle us with migraine headaches, back problems, diabetes, or food allergies. It may even be as life-altering as why He chose for us a life where a handicap limits our potential to become all we want to be.

This question is relevant on many levels, as the Reporter pointed out. But the heart of the matter remains the same: Why am I *this* way? I've asked that many times in the privacy of my prayers. Haven't you?

Within that query lurks an underlying dissatisfaction with the status quo, a vague wondering whether someone else wangled an easier ride through life. Did she get the primo deal, while I got the bargain-basement plan?

In effect we're telling our Creator, *If You'd asked me before You made me, I'd have told You exactly what I wanted to be/become/have.*

I'd have liked to be thinner (*much!*), to have a melodious soprano voice rather than a gravelly alto one, or to become a concert mistress rather than sit hidden in the second violin section. I'd have foregone my food allergies (too many to list) and ditched my migraines. That surgery I had to endure three years ago, I'd have passed on that, too. And that's just for openers. If the plan had been mine, I'm pretty sure this package deal isn't the one I'd have selected.

But the plan wasn't mine, so I got this life when He was handing them out. Just like our friend DD got hers, and you got yours. Was it by accident? Was it an oversight? Were we running late that day and someone else got gourmet lives served picture perfect on bone china platters while we had to make do with leftovers tossed on paper plates?

I see all those implications fueling our friend's *disgruntledness*—and often my own, which is why I suspect I wasn't too far off when I imagined some of Christ's first words to DD as: "You and I both know *Disgruntled* isn't the name you were meant to have." I doubt He has that in the plan for any of us. But how can we move from disgruntled to content, from frustrated to calm, from anger to peace? More to the point, how would Christ answer, and would His answer make enough difference to allow us to move forward?

Way back when I was a searching college student wondering what path God might have for my career, I lit on a truth hidden in the book of Jeremiah that spoke directly to this question. It's since become a trendy verse to quote glibly, but I have the dog-eared study Bible note dated 1984 to prove that I found it before it became a household chant. (Go ahead, carbon date the ink on my old NASB—it'll prove me right.)

Tucked into the story of the way God allowed His people to experience seventy really bad years is a passage (like the one in Micah last chapter), where God speaks directly to His people. Like Micah's quote from Him, this passage contains promise and challenge, encouragement and direction. From His mouth to our ears—if we're listening.

The passage? Jeremiah 29:11 is its centerpiece. But, let's start a few verses ahead and continue a few verses beyond, to get the more complete meaning.

> Thus says the LORD of hosts, the God of Israel, to all the exiles whom I have sent into exile from Jerusalem to Babylon: Build houses and live in them; plant gardens and eat their produce. Take wives and have sons and daughters. . . . When seventy years are completed for Babylon, I will visit you, and I will fulfill to you my promise and bring you back to this place. For I know the plans I have for you, declares the LORD, plans for welfare and not for evil, to give you a future and a hope. Then you will call upon me and come and pray to me, and I will hear you. You will seek

me and find me, when you seek me with all your heart.
(Jer. 29:4–13)

That's a big chunk of Scripture. But as we unpack its key points together, I suspect we'll uncover answers to satisfy our questioning (or even disgruntled) hearts.

There's a Good Plan

"I know the plans I have for you, declares the LORD." Few lines could be packed with more reassurance than the whole of that verse. The Creator knows us and has a plan for us. A good plan. A prosperous plan. A hopeful plan.

According to Young's Literal Translation, the phrase that opens verse 11 could be translated as "I have known the *thoughts that I am thinking toward you*" (emphasis added). This wrinkle adds dimension to our understanding. Personally crafted plans for each one of us began in the mind of God. They're loftier than mortal minds could understand.

Start and stop there, though, and we have an incomplete picture.

For we find in the context of God offering this affirmation that He is speaking to a group sent into exile. Away from their homes. Away from their extended families. Away from their beloved temple of the Living God. It would be that way for more than three generations. Mingled with the magnificent promise is the chilling fact that there would be no easy fix. No early release. This life has been selected for them for the long haul. Who had selected it? God takes full responsibility when He addresses them as those "whom I have sent into exile."

He had a purpose for them during those days—despite, or perhaps because of their plight. Build lives. Celebrate. Pray. Bless and don't curse. Grow. Multiply. Mature. That's the essence of the prophecy's opening. *Don't wallow,* He's telling them. *Don't moan about the fact that other generations enjoyed the land of milk and honey, now you're relegated to a meager existence in pagan territory. I know exactly who you are and where you're living. I planned it just this way.*

David the psalmist demonstrated a powerful knowledge of this truth generations earlier when he crafted the poetic imagery of Psalm 139, with phrases describing the way God was intimately involved in creating him (and by implication us): *wonderfully made* (v. 14), *knitted together* (v. 13), *intricately woven* (v. 15). Consider the life David led—he was the rightful king forced to hide out in caves and make do with a band of misfits as his bodyguard/fighting force. He had to watch as another man won his wife's heart, as his infant son died as a consequence of his own sin, and as his kingship was threatened by enemies both outside and within his household. Then consider that he was the one who acknowledged before God:

> Your eyes saw my unformed substance;
>   in your book were written, every one of them,
>   the days that were formed for me,
>   when as yet there was none of them. (Ps. 139:16)

That is to say, The plan was Yours, God, from the beginning. You crafted me. You prepared my life path. None of it is by chance.

I wonder if the people of Jeremiah's day reflected on David's psalm when they heard the words of the Jeremiah 29:11 promise? They hadn't always been attuned to the voice of God. In fact, when the crisis first loomed, they'd believed their self-appointed false prophets who'd promised captivity could never happen to them. Then, it did happen. The worst they could imagine and more besides. So they fell into despondency. They were inconsolable. At that moment, at the end of themselves, God met them with those words of truth (not sugarcoated falsehoods) and a promise.

I love the way nineteenth-century Bible commentator Adam Clarke explained it in a section he aptly subtitled "Thoughts of Peace":

Here God gives them to understand,

1. That his love was moved towards them.
2. That he would perform his good word, his promises often repeated, to them.
3. That for the fulfillment of these they must pray, seek, and search.
4. That . . . they should find him; provided, they sought him with their whole heart.[1]

God put His finger on the greatest need the people had. They were in turmoil, clinging to an overturned raft in churning whitewater, fighting against the unstoppable current of His plan. They needed to stop flailing and relax to receive the priceless gift of His peace, which is what makes Clarke's peace-bringing points one and two consistent with what we've discovered already: God has something good in mind for us, something lofty and superior, and we'd be well advised to relax into it rather than fight against it.

But what is it?

We Can Find It—But Not Without Effort

The answer leads us to Jeremiah 29:12–14. What could be better for us than to find the Almighty God at the apex of our searches? What good could supersede our finding the pearl of great value (Matt. 13:46), or our thirsts being satisfied at the bottomless fountain of living water (John 4:13–14)?

As long as we, our friend DD, or the people of Jeremiah's day focus on hopelessness, we'll be mired in despondency. But when we take the prescription of verses 12–14 seriously, to call out to God, to pray to God, to seek and seek and seek after Him with every fiber of our being, His promise is unequivocal, spoke in triplicate just in case we don't get it on the first or second telling: "I will hear you" (v. 12); "You will . . . find me" (v. 13); "I will be found by you" (v. 14).

The caveat is that we must be willing to put in the effort. Again, as long as we're tied up in wallowing and bemoaning the unfairness of our circumstances, we'll never be able to corral our energies into an all-out, seek-through-the-night, and don't-quit-until-you-find-Him search for the living God.

The story was plastered all over the news not long ago: sixty-seven-year-old David Lavau, a Los Angeles father and grandfather, hadn't been heard from in several days. His family reported him missing. While authorities soon abandoned their search for him, the man's children refused to give up. The CBS news report quoted the children as saying, "We know our dad. [He] would never not call his kids." They wouldn't sit around and hope. They'd *do* something.

So, they began their search at the last site where he had been, a grocery store where his debit card had been used. His daughter Lisa told reporters, "We stopped at every ravine and looked over every hill, and then my brother got out of the car and we kept screaming and the next thing we heard Dad saying 'help, help,' and there he was." Six days earlier, his car had careened over a five-hundred-foot cliff. He'd survived on leaves and creek water, but only his family's relentless search located him and eventually saw him carried to safety.[2]

When I think of the effort this family put in, against all odds, against all evidence to the contrary—that defines for me seeking with all your heart. If only I would make it my first act in a crisis to keep screaming for God at every ravine and every hill until I find Him.

The beauty of the promise in Jeremiah is that if we put this effort in, we can take it to the bank that we will find God. According to Titus 1:2, any word God speaks is take-it-to-the-bank guaranteed, because He *can't* lie.

So, God's prescription for their years of bondage (Jer. 29:4–9) and I suspect for our seasons of dissatisfaction is: make yourself at home there; be strong; celebrate small victories; try to make things better around you; pray for the people who are suffering with you. Don't let anyone deceive you that there's a shortcut out of this (v. 8). There isn't. But that's okay, because if you look for Me, you will find Me in it.

And Now, Back to Our Interview . . .

Yes. My Disgruntled child, anger and disappointment are your constant companions. Your life is wracked with pain. It is no easy road that I have selected for you. You are right in carrying your anger and frustration to Me. For in the measure of the depths of your pain, in that same measure you will find My resources available to you—and sufficient for you. Those who know only surface pain do not have the privilege of plumbing the depths of My love and sufficiency, as you do.

Really? That's all You have to offer me?

I offer you all I am. I offer you the assurance that I know why I made you. I know the path I have selected for you, and on that path, if you seek Me with everything you have and, everything you are, you will find Me there. No more than what you have is needed; no less than all you have is required.

You mean I should offer You my handicap? My broken-down, less-than-perfect self? Why in the world would You ever want that? C'mon! You're nuts if You think You could find value in all this pain.

I wove you together, after all.

So You made me this way, on purpose? Why should I want to even talk to Someone Who would do that? This interview is over!

No, wait, Precious Child. Yes, I would take you as I wove you together. I would use you to bring glory to My Father. I offer you another promise besides: there is hope for your future. What you see here, today, in the limitations placed on your body, is only temporary. In My Father's house, where I have prepared a place for you, these brief, temporary trials will one day fade into the mist of distant memory. One day you will awaken to find that what I had to offer was more than enough and what I asked in return was more than worth the sacrifice. I give you My word on that. Try Me, see if I don't fulfill that promise to you and more besides.

Discussion Questions

1. List the limitations or circumstances in your life that have you wondering whether God made a mistake in creating you the way that you are.

2. Read and reread Jeremiah 29:4–13. Imagine you were among the people hearing this in the prophet's day. What comfort would you find in God's words? What disappointments would you find? What challenges would there be? What will you decide to do about His direction in verse 5?

3. One key to substituting contentment for disillusionment is to make the conscious decision to seek God with all our hearts. Examine what Jesus said in Mark 12:30. What difference would it make to your personal challenges if you put all your effort into loving God and allotted no energy to wallowing in disappointment?

Chapter 3

When I Fail, Will You Take Me Back?

The control-room intercom is active, and the Producer's side of a conversation booms out across the studio.

Whad-da-ya mean? . . . We're set up to cut live to your feed *now*. . . . I don't want to hear about jackknifed semis or clogged interstates. Those aren't my concern . . . I can't believe you'd be so careless. We have an important Guest here. We can't have Him waiting around for your crew to get your act together. . . . You'd *better* find a way . . . I don't know. Sprout wings . . . No, I'm not out of my mind, but you'll be out of a job if you don't . . .

Midsentence, the sound ceases in the studio. For, in one fluid move, the Reporter has snatched her tablet, nodded to her Guest, dodged snaked cables and shocked production staff, and dashed into the control room. This is one conversation she doesn't want their Honored Guest to witness. No one on the crew wants to witness it, either. They scatter in a millisecond, leaving the Guest calmly seated in His place, and the Floor Director, Gretta, looking more than a little flustered.

Um. Sir? Sorry for this delay. Can I get You something while You wait? More water, perhaps? Or a snack? I'm sure the crew is doing everything they can to . . .

No worries, child. I have more than enough time and an ample supply of everything I require. Will you sit here across from Me? I have been wanting to have time to talk with you.

You have? To *me*? I'd think You'd have lots more important people to meet. I mean I used to be someone worth talking to back when I was the big kahuna of this newsroom, but now, I'm just a glorified gopher—I give the signals, get the mikes hooked up, and make sure guests like Yourself have enough bottled water. I'm really nobody special. They were pretty generous to let me stay on to finish out my contract. No, You don't want me. Who You really ought to talk to is . . .

You are the one on My agenda just now. Sit. Please.

I . . . I guess it'd be okay, if You insist. It does feel good to sit and rest these tired bones. They creak and crackle in places they never used to. Standing so long didn't bother me back in the day. Back then, I also didn't need these goggles to read a script. It's no fun getting older, let me tell You.

With age comes benefit, as well as pain. There is wisdom from lessons learned and respect from years of maturing experience. The plan was always for age to be celebrated and honored.

You can be sure no one is celebrating or honoring me. And I doubt anyone here would accuse me of hoarding a boatload of wisdom or even of learning much from the jams I've gotten myself into.

Will you tell Me about the jams you have been through?

Naw. You don't want to hear about them. Old news. Maybe You could tell me more about Yourself?

Later. Now, I want to hear about you and those jams.

You're a hard One to refuse. I can't believe I'm telling this to You, of all people. Um . . . I was the first woman to earn the rank of station news director here. The money was great, but the power was intoxicating. It grew with each award we earned and each exclusive story we broke. I was invincible. Everyone on my staff—men and women—did what I said. No one dared question me. I made loud demands and fired anyone who didn't measure up—all in the name of excellence, but really all because *I could*. What You just overheard from the control room would be the tiniest whimper by comparison to my tantrums—she learned from *me*. They feared me. They also loathed me.

That happens often.

I didn't check my attitude at the door, either. It wasn't long before my husband seemed like an old bore, so I had an affair with a gorgeous young bartender I let pick me up. After closing time, we'd load up on drinks and occasionally even drugs. They were there for the taking—a forbidden liaison and forbidden substances.

Many are lured by these temptations. Tell me, did you find what you were looking for? Were you satisfied?

It was fun at first—a real rush. I felt like I could see everything clearly. I thought I had it compartmentalized, all under control. But then I made a big mistake on a news story. Really big. I cost the station millions in a defamation suit—all from something I should have caught, should have checked, but I was too busy with my after-hours activities to take the producer's call that night. Just like that, my power, my position, my husband, and my daughter—all gone. Even my young fling lost interest. I'm still shocked that management didn't fire me on the spot. Then again, this purgatory is no picnic. You saw everyone scatter just now? They all used to work for me. Today, not one of them would let me anywhere near their refuges from this or any other newsroom storm. Can't say I blame them. Demoted and disgraced, completely alone and invisible. That's what I've come to.

I see. So, what is your plan to win back respect and to make up for the years you squandered?

There's no plan. There's no chance of any of that.

If you were to ask Me the same questions, you might be surprised that I have an answer—if you *wanted* to ask, that is.

What if we wanted to ask Jesus that question? What if we came to Him with a grungy old sack teeming with all the brokenness and shame of all our consequence-laden sins? What if in dumping the sack at His feet we ask, "I've done all this—and I've been caught at it. Is there anything I can do—or anything You can do—to make things right again? Can You . . . will You take me back?"

Knowing Him as I do, I know He wouldn't mince words. He wouldn't hedge or fudge or say anything warm and fuzzy just to make me feel better. He'd be truthful—and direct. So that's why I believe He'd answer with a one-word command, the one that Matthew records as the first message Jesus preached.

That word? *Repent*.

Jesus began to preach, saying, "Repent, for the kingdom of heaven is at hand" (Matt. 4:17). It's abstract, fairly uncommon for us to use. It can be hard to get a fix on what *repent* means. This word picture may help.

A child who is deathly allergic to peanuts is holding a heaping spoon of crunchy, creamy Skippy near his tongue when he's busted by his mom. Even this proximity to the deadly stuff likely requires a shot to avert anaphylaxis. But the stuff looks good to him. He likes the smooth texture. He hates that he was caught and stopped so near his goal.

His is a dangerous game. This kid could lose his life if he plays it—if he succumbs to the temptation. His mom works hard to impress on him the desperate need for him to stay far, far away from it. He may not get the idea, though, until he finds himself in a screaming ambulance, gasping for air as his throat swells shut. When he does get it, when he begins to understand the seriousness, he has begun the journey of repentance.

According to Bible commentator Adam Clarke, Jesus used a Greek compound verb, *metanoeō* for *repent* to give us the idea "that, after hearing such preaching, the sinner is led to understand, that the way he has walked in was the way of misery, death, and hell."[1] It's rather like our kid finally being sorry he started this whole dangerous drama.

Sorry You Got Caught

The word Jesus used, though, isn't the only New Testament word for repentance. There's a less beneficial brand. According to Matthew Easton, this second verb, *metamelomai*, indicates "regret or even remorse on account of sin, but not necessarily a change of heart. This word is used with reference to the repentance of Judas (Matt. 27:3)."[2] Judas's desperate, tragic end (suicide) didn't lead to the kind of repentance we'd want to emulate.

Judas modeled unhealthy, incomplete repentance. I suspect Gretta in the opening scene had been living off it for a while, as well. She rather liked the shots of adrenaline that came with breaking vows, breaking laws, breaking convention. She felt a tinge of pride for scheming and hiding. She was only sorry when the consequences exploded in fury across her neatly compartmentalized double life. She had regret of course, but she regretted not the deeds but the carelessness that got her caught.

I've been there a time or two myself (maybe not quite so extreme an example), but my heart wasn't any different. Like the other day when I was sneaking a chocolate-covered cherry in the midafternoon, and Mom appeared unannounced. Busted for breaking my diet, eating between meals, and choosing a high-calorie treat. Busted, but not sorry for swallowing the sweet, sticky substance. Just sorry to be caught.

Come on. Be real. You've done the same thing and felt the same partial guilt. When it's falling off the diet wagon one afternoon, it's probably not a huge deal. But when it's a sin of graver consequence, sorry-I-got-caught can be downright dangerous.

For Appearance Sake

The next level of incomplete repentance finds us doing the right things to correct the problem on the outside, where anyone would think we have it all together, but failing to correct the underlying issues.

Often Old Testament prophets, speaking for Almighty God, come up against this failing in the people. In fact, there's a passage in Joel 2 that covers this issue. The key phrase is in verse 13: "rend your hearts and not your garments." Being sorry for appearance sake won't cut it with God.

According to Alfred Edersheim's *Sketches of Jewish Social Life in the Days of Christ*, for a Jew expressing sorrow or grief, "the first duty was to rend the clothes . . . The rent is made standing, and in front; it is generally about a hand-breadth in length."[3] A man or woman was to show sorrow by this method of dress. Everyone would know. And everyone would empathize, even sympathize.

It's just fine if the repentance goes deeper than torn cloth, but the torn garment was meaningless in itself. The prophet tells us clearly that external ceremony isn't God's best goal for us. The greater context in Joel 2 can help us process how to repent before God.

> Let all the inhabitants of the land tremble,
>   for the day of the Lord is coming; it is near,
>   a day of darkness and gloom,
>   a day of clouds and thick darkness! . . .
>   "Yet even now," declares the Lord,
>   "return to me with all your heart,

with fasting, with weeping, and with mourning;
    and rend your hearts and not your garments."
Return to the LORD your God,
    for he is gracious and merciful,
slow to anger, and abounding in steadfast love;
    and he relents over disaster.
Who knows whether he will not turn and relent,
    and leave a blessing behind him . . . ? (Joel 2:1, 12–14)

Here's what's happening. The people of God look like they're serving Him, but their hearts are far from Him. They don't even realize the greatness of the impending danger. So, He speaks through the prophet Joel to warn them:

- *Disaster approaches*: "A day of darkness and gloom that no one could endure."
- *If this worries you at all, there's but one way to survive*: The Lord Himself invites them (and us), "Return to me with all your heart, with fasting, with weeping, and with mourning."
- *Finally, He crescendos with this reminder*: "Rend your hearts and not your garments." This is heart-deep and real—not shallow and showy. That's where repentance God will accept begins.

Inside Out Repentance

So we're starting on the inside and experiencing real sorrow over our failure to meet God's perfect standard. We're seeing our debt far exceeds our ability to repay. Gretta was getting to this point when she admitted there wasn't a thing she could do to make any of this right. Gone was the blustering and bluffing. Gone was the braggadocio of how clever she thought she was. At last she was at the point of agreeing with God that her conduct was blatant, in-His-face rebellion—that she owed a debt to others and to Him. With this came the realization that there was no way she could ever pay this debt.

Only then was she ready to hear from Christ and agree to His terms. *Holman Bible Dictionary* defines this repentant moment:

> What was demanded was a turning from sin and at the same time a *turning* to God. For the prophets, such a *turning* or *conversion* was not just simply a change within a person; it was openly manifested in justice, kindness, and humility (Mic. 6:8 [you remember that passage from Chapter One]).[4]

Why would we turn *to* God with our sin? Wouldn't it be more natural to turn away when we know how deeply we have wounded Him, how odious our sin is to Him? If we were talking about a distant, unknowable god, then perhaps. But not the God of the universe—the Almighty. He made a different way. At a real moment in human history, this God orchestrated a cosmic event of gargantuan proportions.

Jesus Christ lived in human form *perfectly.* He lived one hundred percent perfection without one deviation. As He hung on the cross preparing to breathe His last breath, the balance of His sin account was $0.00. He was unique in this area, because the balance in the sin account of every other human who has ever lived or will ever live is a number way larger than the accumulated national debt of every country on the planet.

In that moment of cosmic transfer, the balance due of insurmountable debt owed by every human soul was moved into the sin account of God's Son, Jesus Christ. His balance went from zero to countless zillions. The apostle Paul explains that He Who knew no sin *became* sin, so that we might become the righteousness of God in Him (paraphrased from 2 Cor. 5:21). With His death, sufficient payment went into His account to cover the entire balance. Every sin, *every* sin was paid in full.

But until a human heart is ready to repent, until each of us reaches the point of petitioning heaven to accept complete payment to cover our blood debt from Christ's account, until then our debt counts against us.

It's been paid. It could be zeroed out. But it won't be, until we ask. When we do at last make this request, our balance is paid in full. Not forgiven with the flip of a switch, but forgiven with the payment of blood for blood, death for death. I owed death for breaking God's law. Christ paid death, although He broke no law. And as Christ picked up His life again in His resurrection, so He offers every repentant heart the opportunity to share in His eternal life.

Repentance—agreeing with God that we don't deserve and couldn't possibly earn forgiveness and turning from our sin toward our open-armed, loving Creator—makes all this possible.

It works two ways. One, it works for the repentant sinner who, for the first time, accepts Christ's complete work on her behalf. Second, it works just as well for the Christian, sullied by brushes with the world and sinful nature, who is in need of turning again from our sin that grieves our Lord. Think of King David writing his passionate song of confession and repentance in Psalm 51: "Create in me a clean heart, oh God, and renew a right spirit within me" (v. 10). It's an apt prayer of repentance for every one of us.

Consequences and Restoration

Will our repentance wipe out the consequences of our sinful choices? Not usually. Not this side of eternity, anyway. The thief beside Christ on the cross, though in his heart repentant, did not receive a reprieve from his sentence of death. Fictional Gretta, wracked with regret, probably will never work her way up to news director again.

Like her, we may be stuck with the consequences of our choices—broken relationships, unplanned pregnancies, legal payment due for against-the-law acts. But where it counts, we, like the hanging thief, will get a permanent reprieve. In heaven's books, his debt and ours can be marked paid in full by the Man hanging beside him.

Perhaps, though this side of eternity, the Lord may in His grace see fit to do what He promised later in Joel's prophecy, "I will restore to you the years that the swarming locust has eaten" (Joel 2:25). Warren Wiersbe quotes great preacher Charles Spurgeon to explain: "You cannot have back your time; but there is a strange and wonderful way in which God can give back to you the wasted blessings, the unripened fruits of years over which you mourned."[5]

And Now, Back to Our Interview . . .

The heated conversation in the control room, visible in mime to Gretta and the Guest, continues. Still, the Guest maintains eye contact with the woman across the table from Him. Finally, she speaks.

Okay. I'll try You. What's Your plan to make up for the years I squandered?

Let Me ask you a question before I answer. How do you feel about what you did?

I'm ashamed, and I'm not afraid to admit it to You. I blew it. For real. If I could erase all those choices and make new ones, I'd do it in a heartbeat. I'd be more understanding to my staff. I'd be more selfless with my husband and daughter. I'd steer clear of anything that makes me out of control. I am truly sorry for how I acted, for what I did.

You are not proud of what you did? Not just sorry you got caught?

Maybe I was at first. But meeting You exploded that façade. I mean, You make me feel like I could be better than all that. Like I was meant for something so much more. I regret that I didn't live up to Your expectations of me. I failed.

That's what I wanted to know. Now, let's talk about making a cosmic transaction that can forgive your sin and set you on a new path—a path you can travel with a brand new life. If you would like, I can help you stop practicing sin. I can help restore to you much of what you lost.

No way! You could do that? You *would* do that? For me? What's the catch?

No catch. It is yours for the asking.

Discussion Questions

1. Why do you suppose John the Baptist and Jesus opened their respective presentations of the good news with the call, "Repent, for the kingdom of heaven is at hand"? Define *repent*. Give an example of what it looks like in your real life.

2. What's the difference between being sorry for the sake of appearance and being repentant in your heart? See Joel 2:12–14 to determine why God requires the internal brand of sorrow for our sins.

3. Be honest before God about your failures. Come to Him in prayer and admit to them. You won't surprise Him, but you will please Him. Journal your feelings as you approach Him, as you listen for His voice of compassion, and as you receive His forgiveness.

Chapter 4

Why Have You Allowed Bad Things into My Life?

The control room door flies open, and the Reporter hurries onto the set. The light on her earpiece glows electric blue. The crew appears and soon is in place. Cameras and monitors come alive. The on-location screen brings up a fashionable brunette, mid-forties, standing on a lush lawn framed by palms with a majestic white and glass structure in the background. She fiddles with an earpiece and lavaliere. A voice from the control room announces,

> Sir, are You ready to roll? We do apologize for the delay, but we have the crew onsite now at the Conservatory of Flowers in Golden Gate Park. Our question will come from someone who gives her name as Flummoxed in Frisco. We're ready to cut live, if You are.

The Guest nods, and the Floor Director starts the countdown. The Reporter dons her screen persona and smiles into the camera.

> Flummoxed, are you there?
>
> Sure am.

It looks like you had a lovely place to wait, at least, as our crew cleared traffic on the Golden Gate Bridge.

I did. Actually, I used the time to enjoy the exotic orchids in the Highland Tropics gallery. Every time I get here I see some variety I've never noticed before, and I do adore orchids.

Thanks for being so gracious! Well, as you know, we have with us in studio a pretty special Guest. I think you'll find Him worth the wait. I know you have an intense question for Him. So I'll step out of the way and let you address Him directly.

My Lord?

Yes, daughter. It is I.

I know they said You'd be there, but I couldn't really believe it. Then with the delay, I figured I was right in assuming it was too good to be true—par for my course, You know? I still can't believe You'd take the time to answer my question. It seems rather impertinent, now that I see You. But, maybe You could help?

Tell Me, treasured one, what has you feeling Flummoxed? What brings you here?

I had this all rehearsed, and suddenly it's all going out of my head. I'm not usually so scattered.

Take your time.

Okay. Breathe in; breathe out. . . . I'm ready. Can they cut that out of the tape? I mean, can they make me look less ditzy? My church friends will be watching the broadcast, and I don't want them to think less of me.

Forget the crew and your church friends; just talk to Me. What is on your heart?

My heart? You would ask about my *heart*? Where have You been these last few months?

I have been right here with you, daughter. But I would like to hear about it from you.

It's crushed. That's what my heart is. My husband of fifteen years abandoned our family. We trusted him—*I* trusted him, and now he's wadded up my heart like an old newspaper and thrown it away—and me with it. Our daughter is fourteen, and she's taking this harder than I am. Her grades are dropping. She's choosing friends who are influencing her to do things she'd never have considered before. Our ten-year-old has type one diabetes. I'm trying to get him used to his new insulin pump. So far it's not working. When I leave here, I have to get him back to his endocrinologist's office. If that's not enough, I got the house in the divorce settlement, but it's worth less than I owe on it—and even if it weren't, I couldn't afford to make the payments—of course, if my ex would pay his child support, we wouldn't be quite so bad off. I'm working as many hours as I can get, but everyone's overtime has been cut, as our company is courting a merger partner. I have to keep this job, because without it I wouldn't have insurance to cover my son's meds. I'm all alone, working myself to exhaustion, thirty days from foreclosure, and responsible for two kids with problems I can't begin to solve. Their father doesn't even come and take them on the occasional weekend.

And you are feeling . . . ?

How am I supposed to feel? I'm Flummoxed. Confused. Angry. Hurt. Can You blame me? I've been a Christian for a lot of years—a pretty good one. I thought You were supposed to bless Your people with peace and abundant life—prosperity, even. What happened to all that for me? Why is all this bad stuff piling up on me? Why are You letting this happen to me?

Before the Guest can respond, the view from the Conservatory lawn begins to destabilize. The sound of tinkling glass feeds through the camera's ambient microphone; from Flummoxed's lavaliere comes a shriek. Camera shots rock and roll as if the tripod has lost its sea legs. Ten seconds into the disturbance, the monitor onsite crashes from its stand. Finally, all is still.

The feed into the studio returns to normal, and Flummoxed's desperate voice is audible.

> An earthquake? On top of everything else? Now, I can't even see You. How could You? How *could* You?

I don't know where they get it—and by *it*, I mean the idea that nothing bad is supposed to happen to Christians, at least not good Christians who have enough faith. Yes, I am aware that in several Scriptures Christ talks about abundant life (John 10:10), about receiving whatever we ask from God (Matt. 21:22), and about the joys that come with serving Him (Matt. 25:23).

Clearly these quotes from our Lord can't mean what popular preachers tell us they mean. It doesn't take much digging into church history to discover that bad things happen to God's best servants. Listen to how Paul described the challenges of his postconversion life. Surely no one could fault Paul for having less-than-adequate faith, yet he recalled:

> Five times I received at the hands of the Jews the forty lashes less one. Three times I was beaten with rods. Once I was stoned. Three times I was shipwrecked; a night and a day I was adrift at sea; on frequent journeys, in danger from rivers, danger from robbers, danger from my own people, danger from Gentiles, danger in the city, danger in the wilderness, danger at sea, danger from false brothers; in toil and hardship, through many a sleepless night, in hunger and thirst, often without food, in cold and exposure. And, apart from other things, there is the daily pressure on me of my anxiety for all the churches. (2 Cor. 11:24–28)

In fact, all the apostles except John were martyred at the hands of grue-some men, and John didn't exactly have it easy according to *AMG's Encyclopedia of Bible Facts:*

> Tradition states that John . . . was boiled in a huge basin of
> boiling oil during a wave of persecution in Rome. However,
> he was miraculously delivered from death. John was then
> sentenced to the mines on the prison island of Patmos
> where he wrote the book of Revelation.[1]

Those stories and thousands of others tell of real believers whose faith connection with God remained intimate and consistent, and yet they were still subjected to unthinkable tragedy. If you read anything at all about the persecuted church (check out www.persecution.com), you'll read story after story about believers in our generation who make the Flummoxed's downward spiral seem positively tranquil.

What gives? Why doesn't God, Who can do anything He chooses, make our lives a peaceful journey toward heaven on life rafts that never spring leaks, never capsize, and never get tossed in violent waves stirred up by hate-filled, powerful people?

Not Alone

As in our earlier questions, I believe at least part of the answer comes from a statement God made to the nation of Israel through one of His prophets. This time, the word comes from God's mouth through Isaiah.

> Fear not, for I have redeemed you; I have called you by
> name, you are mine. When you pass through the waters,
> I will be with you; and through the rivers, they shall not
> overwhelm you; when you walk through fire you shall not
> be burned, and the flame shall not consume you. (Isa.
> 43:1–2)

In that passage, one tiny word appears twice in the original Hebrew. That word? *Kî. When.* Interesting, that the word God chooses isn't *if.* As in—*if* you walk through the fire; *if* you pass through the floods. No! It's a word of certainty—*when.* It also can be translated as *whenever, indeed, even though, because.* The fact is—the floods and fires are coming. That's not a prophetic prediction; it's a definite eventuality. Unwanted, unforeseen, even undeserved trials are going to invade your life and mine. If they're not on the horizon today, be thankful, but don't expect that tomorrow won't be fraught with peril.

That said, though, in making this statement God isn't sitting us down and instructing us to grin and bear it because that's just the way life is. He's saying something different to His people. Look after the *when* statements. If we were to rephrase what He's saying, we might get something like: *Indeed, difficult times are on the horizon for you, but you don't need to fear, because I am with you. My presence with you through the floods (think Moses parting the Red Sea) and the fire (think Shadrach, Meshach, and Abednego in the furnace) means you won't drown in the waters, you won't be consumed by the flames.*

So, I believe the first part of Christ's answer to Flummoxed (and to us) is that you haven't been singled out for tragedy, you haven't earned it (except in the most abstract sense of having been born a sinful citizen of a sin-filled world), and there's not a thing you can do to prevent it. Flummoxed, reading friend, no trial will enter your life except one that happens to others, as well.

Maggie Daley, wife of Chicago's twenty-two-year mayor, learned in 2002 that she had breast cancer. Soon after, she told the media she was shocked, " . . . but you pick up and you move on. . . . I'm not alone here. There are a lot of people who have experienced this."

I find it significant that Maggie's observation is consistent with Paul's statement, "No temptation has overtaken you that is not common to man. God is faithful, and he will not let you be tempted beyond your ability, but with the temptation he will also provide the way of escape, that you may be able to endure it" (1 Cor. 10:13). Paul the shipwrecked. Paul the savagely beaten. Paul the imprisoned. This man affirms that the bitter events that come into our lives are commonplace—everyone has them.

What difference does it make when we fully realize this truth? I think I glimpsed part of the answer as I watched media coverage of Maggie's nine-year battle with the cancer. Maggie was being honored in a ceremony outside a local hospital. While she was at the podium, an ambulance screamed past on its way to the emergency entrance. Maggie stopped her prepared comments and said, "I don't know who's in that ambulance, but I'm praying for them right now." Not only wasn't she surprised that trials had come her way, but she was eager to come alongside others in their suffering. When she died in 2011, the media, her doctors, even her husband's detractors all called her "heroic" and an example to emulate. I'd have to agree.

Better Yet . . .

There's another sense of our companionship in trouble that is even more comforting. Again, look at Isaiah 43. God says clearly, "you don't need to fear, troubled one." Why? Because you belong to Him and He never abandons His own.

The promise here sounds remarkably similar to the one penned by David the poet—a verse often read when comforting the dying. I can't hear it now without recalling how I read it at my grandmother's bedside just moments before she passed into eternity: "Even though I walk through the valley of the shadow of death, I will fear no evil, for you are with me" (Ps. 23:4). Our Lord's nearness in times of trouble is a source of inexplicable peace—of otherworldly comfort.

This is the Lord Who wept over the death of Lazarus. Your suffering is His suffering. "Surely he has borne our griefs and carried our sorrows," Isaiah writes in 53:4. This same sorrow-carrier promises, "I will never leave you nor forsake you" (Heb. 13:5). He walks with us, even carries us, through every storm.

More than simply the negative of not being alone, our fires and floods can reinforce and confirm in our hearts the most powerful truth: God is near the brokenhearted (Ps. 34:18), and we can be sure He will be an ever-present help for us in every trouble (Ps. 46:1).

Consider the lyric to the eighteenth-century hymn, "How Firm a Foundation." You've probably sung it dozens of times, but have you ever noticed that several of its verses are drawn nearly word-for-word from Isaiah 43?

> Fear not, I am with thee; O be not dismayed,
> > For I am thy God, and will still give thee aid;
> > I'll strengthen thee, help thee, and cause thee to stand,
> > Upheld by My righteous, omnipotent hand.
> When thro' fiery trials thy pathway shall lie,
> > My grace, all-sufficient, shall be thy supply;
> > The flame shall not hurt thee; I only design
> > Thy dross to consume, and thy gold to refine.
> The soul that on Jesus hath leaned for repose
> > I will not, I will not desert to his foes;
> > That soul, tho' all hell should endeavor to shake,
> > I'll never, no never, no never forsake!

The English may seem archaic, but the truth is rich and full—God promises He will not desert us and He will never allow all the marshaled forces of hell to shake us loose from His righteous, omnipotent hand. If that's not a better-yet statement, I don't know what is.

God Values the Sufferer

The next part of Christ's answer to Flummoxed, I believe comes in Isaiah 43:4. Here He reassures sufferers that we are "precious" and "honored" in His eyes. I find great courage and comfort to survive and thrive in those statements of affirmation.

Have you ever been tempted to blame God, even to turn on Him? Like a petulant child, I've found my heart crying, *Obviously, You don't like me, or this wouldn't have happened. Maybe I won't like You anymore; maybe I won't even believe in You.*

What a slippery slope. And so misguided. "You are precious in My eyes," He replies to that outburst. How amazing that the mouth of God speaks directly to our raw and aching hearts. Our suffering isn't a negative reflection on our status in His eyes. He isn't letting us know we're on His bad side. He's letting us know that in our suffering, He loves us.

Listen to Him say it to you: He loves you. He thinks of you as precious. The entry on suffering in *The Women's Study Bible* says it best of all:

> God's goodness is nowhere more apparent than in the midst of suffering. His history of providential care and deliverance for His people remains a constant reminder in every generation that He is to carry us *through* every adversity and trial. His presence is sufficient to banish fear. His power is enough to deliver from despair.[2]

It's Not All Bad

Two more short points, and we're done.

First, when God provides the way of escape Paul described in 1 Corinthians 10:13, we tend to talk about it to others. *Wait 'til you hear what God did for me,* we tell anyone with an inclination to listen. And when we do, He receives glory. When we bring Him glory for His provision on our behalf, we fulfill the purpose for which He created us.

Second, walking (or paddling or trudging) through floods and fires offers unique benefits to us. We gain a greater appreciation of His daily blessings as we see the way He provides them in our darkest hours.

That's part of the reason I envisioned Flummoxed taking time to visit the orchid exhibit as she waited for the delayed interview. It illustrates a blending of good with bad—the orchids are around us to enjoy perhaps even more on our toughest days.

We come back to Paul on this matter, too. For he had learned two secrets of contentment despite the string of hazards he endured.

- "But he said to me, 'My grace is sufficient for you, for my power is made perfect in weakness.' Therefore I will boast all the more gladly of my weaknesses, so that the power of Christ may rest upon me." (2 Cor. 12:9)
- I know how to be brought low, and I know how to abound. In any and every circumstance, I have learned the secret of facing plenty and hunger, abundance and need. I can do all things through him who strengthens me. (Phil. 4:12–13)

Notice that in every instance the good that arrives through our trials isn't contingent on the bad stuff vanishing but on the truths about our God that we come to know intimately through and in them. We'll look more at this twist in the next chapter.

Now Back to Our Interview . . .

The Reporter taps the screen of her tablet and in a few seconds has a first-response report on the quake.

Is everyone okay out there? We're getting info here from the newsroom that it was a 5.5, centered forty-ish miles from your position.

Yeah. We're still here. I can't see you in the shattered monitor, but the ground has stopped shivering. But I feel like I need an answer even more from your Guest, if He has anything He *can* say to me.

The Reporter turns to the Guest and nods. She notices His tears and looks away quickly.

My dear Flummoxed. When the ground shifts under your feet, to whom can you look but Me? Look to Me now, for I offer you assurance that I will not abandon you. I offer you the same invitation I once offered the psalmist (Ps. 62:8): Trust in Me always. Pour out your heart to Me; I will always be your refuge.

I sure could use a safe place—a refuge.

If you think back over your life, you will see how many times I have been faithful in providing for your needs.

I suppose. But . . .

But it feels like this time is different, right? Like there is no way I could bring you through this fiery furnace.

Yes.

What would make you think I would change this time? I do not change. When I gave you My word that I would be with you in your darkest hours, I meant it. And I still do.

For sure?

I treasure you. I love you. I will not allow the floods—the financial challenges, the medical concerns, the heart trauma of divorce, the sleepless nights of worry over your daughter and son—to drown you.

Sleepless nights? I didn't say anything about sleepless nights. How did you know?

I am right there with you, even though you can't see Me. Trust Me. Depend on Me. Lean hard on Me. Your circumstances may not change today—maybe not even tomorrow. But I will not fail you. I have said these things to you, that in Me you may have peace. In the world you will have tribulation. But take heart; I have overcome the world (John 16:33).

Discussion Questions

1.   What have you found to be the problem with the popular teaching that once we choose to follow Christ, we'll always be happy, healthy, and prosperous? How do you reconcile this teaching with Jesus' words in John 16:33?

2.   Contrast the practical differences between responding to tough times with a grin-and-bear-it attitude against responding to tough times by finding comfort in God and His promise to support us through our troubles?

3.   Using Paul's statement in 1 Corinthians 10:13, write of a time when God proved Himself faithful to you.

Chapter 5

Why Do Others Get All the Good Gifts?

As the San Francisco taping wraps, the crew in the control room becomes restless. The Production Sound Mixer is obviously in need of a smoke; others pull out smart phones and coffee cups. Reluctantly, the Producer taps her intercom.

> That's morning break, people. We go live again in twenty
> minutes. Do what you need to do, but be quick about it.
> We've gotta make up time. I'm not paying OT on this show! If
> anyone's back late, you're all docked! Scram, get outta here.

The crew disperses, leaving the Guest alone again. The Producer notices that the Guest's blazing guards remain on the outskirts of the room and don't approach to see whether He needs refreshment. As the highest-ranking member of the production team (and the only one left on set), she supposes she'll have to do what they ought to be doing for such a high-profile person, if they were employees worth their pay. She walks to the snack table and addresses Him from across the room.

If You need to stretch, now's the time. We'll have a tough interview in studio before we break for lunch. Do You want something? A cup of tea, perhaps?

Tea? Yes, that would be nice—if you would have a cup with Me.

I have a thousand things to . . .

If you would rather not . . .

No, I guess I can spare a minute for You. How do You take it?

With milk and honey, please.

The good stuff, huh?

Nothing but the best and purest.

Yeah, I get it that You take all the good stuff for Yourself—all powerful people do. But what about spreading a bit of it around to the little people—like me? When You handed out the best breaks and prettiest gifts in life, You conveniently skipped me. I got nothin' at all.

That sounds like an accusation. Would you care to elaborate?

You bet I would. It's been like this forever—You oughta know—You picked out my family. I sure didn't have any say in it. My older sister was smarter and prettier. So, all I got in school was, "Why don't you study hard like your sister?" and "Why don't you fix yourself up like your sister so the boys will notice you?" And at home, my little brother got all the breaks just because he was the son my father wished I'd been. No one ever missed his art exhibits or trumpet competitions. But me, I got nothin'. No looks. No smarts. No artistic opportunities. Just, "Do something with yourself, kid. Fix yourself up."

Are you sure you are remembering this as it happened? While I recall those scenes that saddened your young heart, I recall many others that brought you joy and accomplishment—like when your peers elected you editor of your school yearbook. Or, when your junior project in TV production club won broadcast story of the year at the national convention, and when your debate coach selected you as a delegate to the student congress in Washington, DC.

Well, yeah, there was that. But no one from my family bothered to see me in those things. Anyway, then I did something for myself, like they were telling me to. I put myself through college. It took me six years because I had to stop a few times to earn more money, but I graduated with a major in TV production. I worked every freebie internship I could get. It was tough, because I also held down paying jobs so I could eat. And when I did finally graduate, the best I could do was land a crummy job here at this podunk station nobody's ever heard of. It's taken me five years to claw my way up to producer—no thanks to anyone but me.

That is an awfully arrogant comment. Many individuals built into you, helped you become the professional you are today. Many believed in you and opened doors for you.

Really? All I know is that every time there's an award to be given out, my best work is ignored—I don't even get nominated so I can act all humble and say what an honor it is to be considered. And every time there's a network opening, it always goes to someone less qualified but from a larger market where they get more attention.

Interesting, how you perceive your life. I believe you are working up to a question for Me?

All right, whaddaya say to this? If You own the flocks on a thousand hills, if it all belongs to You, why don't You share some good gifts with me instead of just tossing me smelly old scraps? If goodness and mercy really follow You, why don't I get any?

I have several friends who've made it big in their industries—so big that their multi-figure earnings have been widely publicized. What invariably happens is that instead of people in their circles being happy for their successes, they become jealous—and greedy. One friend tells of total strangers (to say nothing of those closer to her) contacting her out of nowhere, demanding that she take the wealth she earned and spread it around to their pet causes. Some even try to make my friend feel guilty for the success her hard work and God's blessing have netted her. Rather audacious, if you ask me.

But according to the old-time Puritan preacher Jonathan Edwards, we have the same attitude toward God when we accuse Him the way the Producer did in our interview. Here's what Edwards wrote in a sermon on the justice of God:

> Is not God worthy to have the same right, with respect to the gifts of his grace, that a man has to his money or goods? . . . If any of you see cause to show kindness to a neighbour, do all the rest of your neighbours come to you, and tell you, that you owe them so much as you have given to such a man? But this is the way that you deal with God, as though God were not worthy to have as absolute a property in his goods, as you have in yours.[1]

Doesn't God, Who reigns supreme over the entire universe, have the absolute right to determine which gifts He gives to each of us? Even the choice of whether or not to give any gift at all sits entirely in His hands. And yet, He does give—freely, abundantly, overflowingly, graciously, lovingly. Because it is His nature to do so—it is His *choice* to do so.

Ah, there's the rub, as Hamlet might say. Since He gives so much, we assume we are entitled to it all, as if the right belonged to us in the first place. Here's the news bulletin of the day—it doesn't belong to us; it never did. Listen to the words Paul penned as a reminder to those of us intent on demanding our rights before the Holy God: "What do you have that you did not receive? If then you received it, why do you boast as if you did not receive it?" (1 Cor. 4:7). Entitlement is a dangerous outlook. It leads to laziness, to anger, and to all manner of unhealthy habits.

Refresher on What God Requires

Fact is, though, that God does give His solemn word that He will bless those who make the choice to follow Him. From His mouth, reported through the prophet Isaiah, we read: "Thus says the LORD: 'Keep justice, and do righteousness, for soon my salvation will come, and my righteousness be revealed'" (Isa. 56:1). What follows that word of promise is a description of the over-the-top gifts He will give to two groups of people who make the costly choice to align themselves with Him.

We'll look at the gifts He promises in a moment. But first, I notice something that perhaps you picked up, as well. The terms of the promise remind me of our discussion in Chapter One.

What does God want from us? That we act in justice, exercise mercy, walk in humility before Him. (The humility portion of the reminder comes in verse 2, where it is exhibited in *submitting* to God's law.) His requirements are remarkably consistent throughout Scripture. On this point, though, it looks like we needed a refresher since our sense of entitlement tends to entice us away from the traits God asks us to exhibit.

Justice. Mercy. Humility. These flow *to* us as gifts from God, and ought to flow *out* of us toward others with equal abundance. Remember the parable Jesus told about the slave forgiven of an insurmountable debt? After being forgiven that debt, he immediately goes out and shakes down his fellow slave for a pittance owed. Jesus' strong condemnation ought to give us pause: "You wicked slave! I forgave you all that debt because you begged me. Shouldn't you also have had mercy on your fellow slave, as I had mercy on you?" (Matt. 18:32–33 HCSB).

One of the first things we notice about the Producer in the drama is that she lacks these traits. Her sense of justice is me-centered; she is merciless with her staff; she wears her haughtiness like a badge of honor; she demands blessings of God, as if she had them coming.

I've made these traits blatant for the sake of illustration. (Also, I've chosen not to give her a name because she defines herself by what she does rather than who she is.) Yet which of us can't relate? I have a long list of gifts I want God to give me. It gets longer when I look around at other people. They have this possession *I want*, this relationship *I want*, this job *I want*. Quickly I deteriorate to whininess, telling God that since He gave these gifts to others, He owes them to me as well.

Yet gifts, by their very nature, are at the discretion of the giver.

Let me illustrate. Back in my mom's day, a bride-to-be picked out her china pattern and perhaps listed the colors of her kitchen and bathroom, but gifts selected for her bridal shower were at her guests' discretion. They reflected the personality of the giver and the depth of her relationship with the bride. But today, a bride registers at her favorite stores for everything from kitchen appliances to vacuum cleaners to the garden tools she wants for her new home. With great care, she picks out her own gifts and tells her guests what to bring to her party. We've removed the personality and relationship aspect of the giver in the gift.

I suspect many of us would like to deal that way with God—choose our gifts from a list of those in His storehouse and invite Him to our party as long as He brings one of the most costly items from our list.

The Greatest Gift Already Given

Back in Isaiah 56:1, we read of the gift God prizes most highly, perhaps because of its unsurpassable cost to Him and the substantial way it expresses His personality as the Giver. We find it in the phrase that explains why He demands we remain just and righteous: "for soon my *salvation* will come" (emphasis added).

When I managed the editorial department at Moody Publishers, I had the privilege of meeting Charles Ryrie, whose *Ryrie Study Bible* we published. During our association there, I came to hold Dr. Ryrie in deep respect. So, whenever I see that he has a comment on a topic, I pay special attention. In his book *Basic Theology*, Dr. Ryrie explains this gift:

> Why should God want to save sinners? Why should He bear the pain of giving His only begotten Son to die for people who had rebelled against His goodness? . . . This was the greatest and most concrete demonstration of the love of God. His good gifts in nature and through His providential care (great as they are) do not hold a candle to the gift of His Son to be our Savior. John 3:16 reminds us that His love was shown in His gift, and Romans 5:8 says that God proved conclusively that He loved us by the death of Christ.[2]

I like several phrases in that comment. First, that God does give us tangible, good gifts through the natural world and through His providence. But these "do not hold a candle" to salvation—the pinnacle gift, the loving gift that answers and supplies our greatest need.

Dr. Ryrie refers to two Scriptures familiar to us: Romans 5:8, which tells us that God's gift came when we least deserved it (while we were still sinners), and John 3:16, which tells us that out of His deep, abiding love, God *gave* the gift closest to His heart. There is no greater gift than one that costs the Giver everything. In God's case, it cost the life of His only Son.

The Promise of Blessings

Returning to Isaiah 56, we notice next the promise God makes is to people who do something—who keep His laws and align themselves with His cause. God is saying that special blessings flow from His hand to those who join themselves to Him. These people (the eunuchs and the foreigners in verses 3–7) made crucial choices in humbling themselves, in giving themselves wholly to God, and in not caring that it would cost them what others would consider normal—children, family ties, earthly connection. In verse 4, God calls the eunuchs those "who choose the things that please" Him. The foreigners He calls out for ministering to Him, loving His name, and becoming His servants (v. 6).

The blessings He promises are to give them in abundance far more than they have given up. For the eunuchs, He promises a heritage better than sons and daughters, an everlasting name. For the foreigners, He promises to enfold them into the holy family of priests who have the privilege of offering sacrifices acceptable to Him.

These are gifts only the Creator is able to offer. Only He can work outside the laws of nature or of birth. Doesn't this remind you of Jesus' promise, "There is no one who has left a house or wife or brothers or parents or children, for the sake of the kingdom of God, who will not receive many times more in this time, and in the age to come eternal life" (Luke 18:29–30)?

The Measure of Blessings

I suppose we need eyes trained to see the gifts we do have—those we have already received—rather than those we are so desperate to obtain but may have no business having. Perhaps our measure of blessings needs to be recalibrated, like a scale that's off its absolute zero. Let's dial back to zero and see the great distance God has brought us.

Listen to Ephesians 1:3: "Blessed be the God and Father of our Lord Jesus Christ, who has blessed us in Christ with every spiritual blessing in the heavenly places." It would seem that God would have us use a different measure entirely—one calibrated to eternity rather than to this temporary world.

So, then, are you looking at the list of things others have and you want? Or, are you looking at the far longer, more valuable list of all the undeserved gifts of life and love and eternity that the God of Love has graciously poured into your hands? Where your eyes are trained will make all the difference in your perspective.

And Now Back to the Studio . . .

The Guest looks away for a long moment, choosing His words carefully. His eyes narrow, belying both obvious pain and restrained anger. He rubs the reddened scars on His wrists. Across the room, His guards' sabers glow brighter, hotter. At last, He turns to the Producer, who is looking at her watch and calculating how much time remains in the break she gave her crew.

So, you consider all the abundant gifts I have given you to be "smelly old scraps"? The life I breathed into you. The ability to learn and earn money and do a job that has value to the community—those you toss into the rag heap? The opportunity to have relationships with other people. A lovely place to live. Enough money to buy showy cars and a fashionable wardrobe. All scraps not worth throwing to the dogs sitting at My feet at the supper table?

Yeah—when you compare them to what my classmates got.

And My scars, which I took on willingly so you wouldn't have to pay the death penalty you owe, they are nothing to you? My offer to you to be saved from My Father's wrath and rescued from eternal punishment? That is worth nothing to you?

Ummm.

You demand goodness and mercy for yourself. What have you done for those around you out of the resources I have given you? What mercy have you shown to others? What humility have you exhibited? What justice have you offered to someone else, when it was in your power?

I've done plenty of good around here—more than anyone deserves!

No! My measure of your heart does not align with your assessment. I do shower blessings—providential blessings—on those who believe in Me and those who do not. You have benefited from these and more besides. But you must know that My best storehouse of blessings—those that last when everything you grasp has long since rusted away—is reserved for those who choose the things that please Me and consider valuable My offer of salvation. As long as you consider these to be scraps and rags, you will receive no more from My hand.

I'm just not buying it. You give me my promotion to the network—and all the good trappings that go with it—then we'll talk.

Discussion Questions

1. Describe a time when you felt life (or God) wasn't being fair. What led you to that conclusion? If you directed your accusation at God, how do you suppose He would respond? What makes you think that?

2. How do Paul's words in 1 Corinthians 4:7 debunk the idea of entitlement that pervades society? How does this myth invade your thoughts about your rights? Why is this a dangerous presumption?

3. Consider Habakkuk's choice (Hab. 3:17–18) to rejoice in God and in salvation despite a world in chaos. How would you go about making this choice? What difference would it make if you did?

Chapter 6

Why Do Answers Take So Long?

The Producer is quick to return to the sanctuary of her control room, and the crew returns to the set. The Reporter addresses the Guest as she takes her seat again.

Sir, I'm looking through my notes, and I see we've scheduled our next interview to be live in studio. I'm told the questioner is in the green room—has been waiting there for over an hour. Her daughter drove her one hundred miles to see You. We were willing to send a crew to her, especially given her age and frailty, but she insisted. She's asked us to call her Weeping in Westdale.

I have known for some time that Weeping has wanted to see Me. Please, let us not delay any longer. Bring her in and make her comfortable.

A side door into the studio opens and a cameraman steps aside to reveal a gray-haired woman leaning heavily on a chrome walker. She totters and grabs on tighter as the split-open tennis balls covering two of the four wheels catch on the slick floors. Behind thick glasses, red-rimmed eyes rise and flicker with hope as they meet the Guest's gaze. Her pace quickens when He extends His arm. He rises to help her get seated. The Floor Director switches on the lavaliere microphone woven discretely through the woman's flowered dress. Instead of sitting, though, Weeping removes her right hand from the walker and grips the Guest's extended arm.

You've got to come with me! Now! Lord, it's my granddaughter. I've been praying for her for twenty-seven years, since the day I learned she was coming into the world. But all my prayers have come to nothing. Now she's lying in a hospital dying, and even yet she still won't listen to reason and put her faith in You. *I'm* ready to die, and that's okay. I've lived a long life—I've served You for near eighty-five years, since I was seven years old. I've been glad to do it. It has been my joy. But my granddaughter doesn't serve You; she isn't ready to die. She won't spend eternity with You. You've got to make her see. Come! Now! We may be able to make it before she . . .

Please, child. Slow down. Sit. Be comfortable. We can talk about this.

It's just so urgent, don't You see? You've got to show her Yourself. It's nearly too late already.

No, not too late. Do you not believe that I hold your granddaughter in My hands, even as I hold you?

I want to believe. Please, Lord, help me believe.

Did someone say earlier that your daughter drove you? Is she in the green room now?

Sure, she's there, but it's her little girl losing life by the minute. My daughter is inconsolable. I invited her to come in, but she said she didn't feel up to seeing You. We're different in that. She can't bear to see You; I *had* to see You.

Would someone tell her I am calling for her?

The Floor Director complies. After several minutes, the studio door opens again, this time revealing a younger version of Weeping, dressed in khakis and a light blue shirt, salt-and-pepper hair swept back in a chignon. One

*camera pans to her and follows her. A production assistant hastily places
a third chair on the set. Once seated and fitted with a microphone, the
younger woman lets her purse slide off her shoulder and land with a
thump, then takes a sip of water. Her eyes don't meet the Guest's, but she
does address Him.*

> Master? You wanted to see me? I've been calling for You for
> years, and You haven't come. Now, You want me to come to
> You? Now, when there's nothing left to be done You suddenly
> decide to pay attention? If You'd gotten involved sooner . . . if
> you'd stopped my headstrong daughter from her destructive
> ways . . .

> Tell me, beloved, do you have a photo of your lovely child?

> Yes, right here in my purse. It's on my phone. You must realize,
> it was taken before . . .

> Of course. May I see?

*As the younger Weeping hands over her smart phone, a sob escapes the
Guest's lips and soon His tears fall freely. Mother and daughter stare
momentarily before losing their composure and matching Him tear for tear.
The Reporter and her crew try to look away—but keep being drawn back
by compassion flowing like an electrical current around the conference
table. No words pass for several minutes. At last, He hands back the phone.*

> She is a lovely young woman—so full of potential
> and opportunity.

> Not now. She's dying in a bed of regret, with no hope of a
> future—here or in heaven. Didn't my mother tell You all that?

> My beloved, you see such a limited view. I see so much more
> than you could imagine. And what I see at this moment is that
> you and your mother have a question for Me. Please, one of
> you, ask.

> Oh, Lord, after all these years, I still am not any closer to
> understanding You. Tell me, please, why do You wait so long

to answer? Why do answers to our most important prayers too often take a lifetime to come—and sometimes even then . . . ?

What my mother means is: Master, don't You care enough to grant our request? Don't You love us, love *my little girl,* at least as much as we do? We've served You faithfully. So, why are You making us wait so long?

I've started this chapter twice. The first version was, well, whiny. That's the kindest word I could use. For of all the questions in this book, this question of waiting is nearest to *my* heart. It's the one, of all, to which I have the fewest consoling answers. So, I moaned about writing it. I moaned about all the waiting I've had to do—all the waiting I continue to do. I moaned about feeling like moaning. It wasn't just a little, mini-moan. It was a full-blown mega-moan. And the one thing it *wasn't* was pretty.

When I was a kid, my mom tried to break me of this habit. But I'm just too good at it. She used to call me *Moan-a* Lisa—which I hated. She'd threaten that if I wanted to moan, she'd give me something to moan about. (Meaning a not-so-friendly whap on the backside.) So I drove the moaning inside, but I couldn't rid myself of it.

This chapter, in its first incarnation (the moaner version), sat open and unfinished on my computer for nearly a week.

As I write now (the second time around), it's approaching Christmas, which is what drew me out of my moan, although not for the reasons you might imagine. It had nothing to do with tinsel or holly or music of the season. But it did have everything to do with two words relating to the birth of Christ, spoken in the core of my being. I didn't hear them with my ears, but I might as well have. It was the voice of my Savior: "*I* waited." *He* waited? Really?

This caused me to reconsider the Christmas story. When and how did Christ wait?

First (and longest), Christ waited down through history—from the creation of the world (Rev. 13:8). He waited for the time to be right to begin the events of His incarnation. In the Old King James version, Paul called this wait, "the fulness of time" (Gal. 4:4).

Then Christ waited nine long months confined to a womb, until again the place and time were right (Luke 2:6). He waited from helpless babyhood through adulthood—thirty years of waiting (Luke 3:23). He waited forty days in the wilderness for the temptation of the enemy to have its wallop at Him (Luke 4:2). He waited through years of ministry, as the disciples would sometimes "get" it and sometimes fail miserably (Matt. 8:26; 16:23).

He waited through a betrayal, a mock trial, a brutal beating, and hours of hanging on the cross (Matt. 26–27). He waited and waited until that one moment, when He summoned His last gasp of earthly breath (John 19:30) to call out the victorious one-word declaration: *Teléō* . . . It. Is. Finished! Or, to put it another way: the wait is over at last.

I guess He did do more than a fair amount of waiting. And so, in our waiting, I guess we're in the best company.

The Complaint

Maybe you think you have the answer to waiting, or maybe you know what you think the answer ought to be. I've heard the clichés, too. God isn't slow to act, as we humans consider slowness (2 Pet. 3:8–9) because to God one thousand years is like a day and a day is like one thousand years.

Well, at least the last part seems true enough. Haven't you had a few of those thousand-year days? Waiting to hear results of a biopsy? Waiting for a family member to turn his life around? Waiting for a job to materialize in a hopeless economy? Waiting for the scales of justice to prevail against someone who's stolen your possessions or livelihood or health or peace of mind? Waiting for money to cover bills? Waiting for God to step in and do something miraculous, despite indisputable evidence that all is lost?

Waiting. And hoping. Until hope is worn to shreds like last decade's blue jeans.

Yet, if Christ does understand how long it seems between our requests and His answers (if He carried our grief and bore our sorrow, He *must* understand), then why do we continue to wait?

This reminds me of the prophet Habakkuk. (Habba-who?) It's a crazy-sounding name, but it means "a wrestler" in ancient Hebrew. His three-chapter book opens with our question of the hour: "O LORD, how long shall I cry for help, and you will not hear?" (Hab. 1:2).

The wrestler sees tragedy on the horizon. Violence is going unpunished. The law is ignored, and justice is miscarried. The wicked are succeeding in stamping down the righteous. And he's wrestling with the reality of why God is allowing this to continue—and for *so* long.

Then the Lord answers, but it's not what Habakkuk expects—or wants to see happen. What he hears (vv. 5–11) is that God is going to allow an even more evil society to overrun His people in punishment for their sinfulness. The God of justice does see these abominable deeds, and He won't let them go unpunished. It's going to get worse before it gets better, Habakkuk. Remember, God's ways are not our ways.

Obviously, this troubles the good prophet. He wants to see evil uprooted without hurting the righteous along with it (think of Daniel, Shadrach, Meshach, and Abednego, whose ancestors are coming up in that culture).

So, in chapter 2, Habakkuk plants himself before God again—and complains—and waits. "I will take my stand at my watchpost and station myself on the tower," he says, "and look out to see what he will say to me and what I will answer concerning my complaint" (v. 1).

Standing Firm

Okay. Habakkuk and I (and you?) needed to get that whining out of our systems. Sometimes we just need to hear ourselves out loud to hear how temper-tantrum-ish we sound. Only in that frame of mind are we ready for verse 2: "And the LORD answered me." At last, He comes. Like our mother and grandmother in the opening story, after what seems like forever, we get our audience with the King.

We can read the full chapter to hear God's full answer, but what's most relevant to us is a key line in verse 4: " . . . the righteous shall live by his faith." It's as if He's saying, *Trust Me, Habakkuk. Trust Me, child of the twenty-first century. Stake your life on faith in Me. When you don't want to wait and you don't understand My purposes, trust Me anyway.*

The writer of Hebrews casts fresh light on this passage:

> Therefore do not throw away your confidence, which has a great reward. For you have need of endurance, so that when you have done the will of God you may receive what is promised. For, "Yet a little while, and the coming one will come and will not delay; but my righteous one shall live by faith, and if he shrinks back, my soul has no pleasure in him." But we are not of those who shrink back and are destroyed, but of those who have faith and preserve their souls. (Heb. 10:35–39)

Here we have the first part of our answer. Our faith needs exercise. Remember that line, "without faith it is impossible to please [God]" (Heb. 11:6). We need faith—strong faith—exercised faith—which comes through endurance, through waiting to receive from God. He gave us the faith muscle, but, like all our muscles, it starts out flabby. It's our responsibility to see that it gets the opportunity to become strong. Sometimes that means taking on the muscle challenge of waiting.

I hate exercise. Truly hate it. I hate it almost as much as I hate waiting. I get on my treadmill on the odd day that I can't manufacture an excuse not to, and I feel like someone's lab rat on a wheel in my cage. While I'm walking in place on my conveyor belt, I'm living only for the moment the bell will ding to indicate my time has been served.

Just as the treadmill is necessary for my physical health, so strong faith in God is necessary for my spiritual health. That means waiting. God may make us wait—long—so we'll get the benefit of learning the lesson of living in complete dependence on Him—to build up that flabby faith muscle.

The good news is the delay may be long, but not forever. In both Habakkuk 2:3 and Hebrews 10:37 we see God promise that He "will not delay." It's not gratuitous waiting. It's not waiting with no end in sight. It's waiting, like Christ showed us, until the time is right from God's perspective.

Get Busy in the Meantime

My next observation comes from the first words God speaks to Habakkuk: "Write the vision; make it plain on tablets, so he may run who reads it" (2:2). I read that as, *be productive in the waiting*. The prophet is supposed to prepare the coming message for those who need to hear it. Since I'm a writer, I especially like that what God tells His man to do in the waiting period is to write.

In our case, the command of what to do may be different, but the principle is clear: don't sit around grumbling about waiting. This may not get us closer to the *why*, but it has everything to do with our attitude and productivity during the elapsed time.

I like the way Paul puts it: "Suffering produces endurance, and endurance produces character, and character produces hope, and hope does not put us to shame, because God's love has been poured into our hearts through the Holy Spirit who has been given to us" (Rom. 5:3–5).

Instead of fighting the wait—grumbling and mumbling and moaning about it—we can turn our eyes to the blessing in the waiting—the purpose and plan for it.

Habakkuk models for us how we ought to be conducting ourselves during the wait. In 3:16 and following, the wrestler has lain down on the mat, exhausted from the match and ready at last to declare: "Yet I will quietly wait." Not wait because I have to. Not wait with gritted teeth. No. I will *quietly* wait. I will be at peace with the waiting.

And while he's waiting, he proclaims with newly exercised faith muscles, "Yet I will rejoice in the LORD; I will take joy in the God of my salvation" (v. 18).

Now, Back to Our Interview . . .

With a scarred hand on each woman's shoulder, the Guest addresses the sobbing mother and daughter.

Daughters, I heard your prayers even before you uttered them. I know it seems I have delayed. But I assure you it is not because I do not care. My Father has a plan and a purpose. You cannot see it now, but that does not make it less real. Do you remember the story of Mary and Martha after their brother Lazarus died? They came to me with the same spirit of disappointment that you have. "Master if You had been here . . . " they both said (John 11:21, 32). You have done right in bringing your child to Me. Now quietly wait until I work in the situation for your good, for her good, and for My Father's glory.

Just then, the younger Weeping's phone rings; she hasn't realized that she's been clutching it since the Guest asked to see her daughter's picture. She jumps at the sound, then glances down to the caller ID and gasps.

It's the hospital. Hello? This is. What? What do you mean? You can't be serious . . .

What is it, beloved?

She's rebounded . . . and she's asking to see her grandmother.

Discussion Questions

1. The words from Daniel 10:10–14 offer a glimpse of what may be going on in the spiritual realm when you pray. What difference does it make to you that God hears your requests "from the first day"?

2. What do we gain from being as persistent in prayer as the prophets Habakkuk and Daniel? Give an example from your life of a situation when waiting for God's answer proved fruitful.

3. God's message to Habakkuk opened with a direction to get busy as he waited. If you're in a waiting season now, what do you believe God would have you do as you wait? How do you know?

Chapter 7

Are You at Work Even When I Can't See You?

While Weeping the younger and Weeping the elder leave the studio, the Producer announces a sixty-minute lunch break. Instantly, the crew scatters. One camera operator hangs back. When he surmises that no one made provision for the Guest's lunch, he approaches and holds out a hand in greeting.

Sir, hi there. Um, the guys call me Cam—I guess You know that. So, um, if You don't have plans for lunch, I'd be honored if You'd share mine with me. It's just a tuna sandwich and a bag of bagel chips, but it's Yours if You'd like it.

Thank you. I will count it a privilege to share your meal with you.

I don't have a desk or anything. But we can sit out of the hot lights at the snack table. It's cooler there—a little more comfortable. Would You like to say the blessing?

I would be happy to do that. Our Father, for Your bountiful provision we thank You. For the generosity of this, My brother, in sharing what He has, I ask You to bless him abundantly and meet the desires of his heart. Amen.

Amen! Although You might want to rethink that "bountiful" part. My wife wasn't feeling well this morning, so I packed this myself. She makes better lunches, and now I double-wish she'd been the one to do it. I didn't imagine I'd be here across the table from You. I would have gotten up earlier to make something worthy of You—'course with me that would have meant getting up a week ago Tuesday.

This is more than fine. I love fish. It reminds me of days spent eating with other friends and brothers by the Tiberias seaside after a night and morning of fishing.

Those sound like special times. Do You miss those days by the sea? Those friends?

Oh, I see them often—in a different place, of course. But there is something special about breaking bread together that bonds us. We held many deep discussions over a meal. That may have been My favorite part.

Do You mean that?

I do.

I was thinking . . . I haven't wanted to presume on Your time, and I'd understand if You were too tired from the morning to get into a discussion with me. I want You to know that I didn't share my lunch just to get Your ear, and really it's okay if You don't want to . . .

I was hoping you would bring it up. Tell me, how is your lovely wife? You said she was feeling poorly?

That's the thing. It's not physical. That way, she's fine. But she's so sad. So empty. Today she called in sick because she couldn't bear to spend another day at the center. She loves counseling the girls, of course, and helping save the lives of those precious babies, but at the same time it breaks her heart.

Your wife does a work that brings great honor to My Father. I am so pleased with her selflessness. I am pleased with you, too, for supporting her as she volunteers.

She'll be glad to know You feel that way.

Do you suppose she might join us?

I doubt it. I mean she was so low this morning that she made me promise not to bother with asking You anything. Obviously, I broke my promise 'cause here we are.

Hmm. Tell Me what is happening on the adoption front.

That's easy. Exactly nothing. We've had our home studies done for three years now. We've interviewed with more agencies than I remember. We got close with adoption—funny that it was during our third round of fertility treatments. We had so much hope—two chances to be parents. We even decorated a nursery in green, so it didn't matter whether it was a boy or a girl. Then the treatments failed, and the birth mother kept her child. A few months later, another hope was dashed with another agency. So, our arms and cradle were empty again—and again. We'd be loving parents—honest, we would. We'd teach the child to know You. We'd provide a warm home and a good education.

And tuna fish sandwiches?

Oh, no! The food would be much better than this crummy sandwich. My sweetheart is a great cook. And we have so many hugs to . . .

The studio door opens, and Cam stops midsentence. A petite redhead carrying a cardboard box filled with pastries steps in. She spots her husband and starts talking before noticing his lunch companion.

Hey Cam, I hope you don't mind but the recording light was off, so I thought I'd see if I could find you. I can only imagine the lunch you packed yourself, so I thought a sweet treat from Italian Bakeshop would make it go down a little better.

Sweetheart, this is great. I've just been having lunch with our Honored Guest. My Lord, I want You to meet my wife. Of course, You know her but . . .

I am so glad you decided to come. We have been talking about the trial you two have been enduring.

And I see that my husband has been subjecting You to one of his tuna fish concoctions?

We have enjoyed our lunch together. But more than that, we have enjoyed fellowship. Sit and join us in a pastry. Perhaps you have something you would like to ask while I am here?

My Lord, I dare not ask. I'll sound ungrateful. You'll think I don't appreciate everything You've given me. I really shouldn't have come. You two enjoy the pastries.

Please, stay—and ask. I will not think any less of you for being honest with Me. You have My word.

Really? . . . I . . . That is to say, we . . . our dream has died. Our dream of being a loving family—one like everyone else. Our dream of a home bubbling with the giggles of children. Is there any hope, or should we just give up? Is Your answer once and for all no, or are You working on something we can't see?

S hould I just give up hope or is the Creator God orchestrating some answer that I can't sense or touch or hear or see? He *could* do it—we know that. But the question is *will* He do it? Cam and his wife give voice to an issue that will plague most of us in some season of life. For them, it's about the dream of parenthood killed by circumstances beyond their control. For others of us, it is about the hopeless collapse of relationships, health, careers, or finances.

Regardless, we stand on a precipice without options. Our feet are perched on the end of all that is humanly possible. The canyon drops off a millimeter from the tips of our toes. The ground has crumbled away behind us. There is no going back, no going forward, and no chance we'll sprout wings to fly to safety. So here we stand—trepidation multiplying and balance wavering above what John Bunyan (of *Pilgrim's Progress* fame) called the Slough of Despond. And once we fall into it, like Bunyan's Christian, all the baggage we carry will weight us down and force us to sink into its murky depths.

What would God say to us in these moments of despair? I searched through many passages in the prophecies God gave to ancient Israel to find a possible answer. To address the specifics of our fictional couple's question, I saw that God eventually provided a child to several childless couples: Abraham and Sarah (Gen. 17), Samuel's parents Hannah and Elkanah (1 Sam. 1), John the Baptist's parents Zechariah and Elizabeth (Luke 1).

But God doesn't speak that same promise to every couple. So, considering His provision for these three as typical wouldn't be prudent.

As I read, I came to understand that the struggle flows from the fact that He doesn't always give us what we want. We can't offer some magical incantation to compel Him to heal us, to restore our fortunes, or to give us the gifts that regular folks all around us seem to enjoy with no unusual effort. Sadly for us, sometimes He answers our prayers with a firm refusal—not right for you, even though it may be perfectly fine for most other people.

My search through the prophecies eventually led me back to Isaiah 43, which we began examining as an answer to Flummoxed's question in Chapter Four. You'll recall that the opening of this prophecy is a marvelous statement of comfort for God-believers who would need to pass through the waters and the fire—and who needed to know God would lead them through bad times.

But there's more to the chapter and to this prophecy than we examined earlier. So, I turned my attention toward the second half of chapter 43—especially verses 16–19. Let's read them together, then I'll unpack what I learned from them about God's invisible hand at work.

> Thus says the LORD, who makes a way in the sea, a path
> in the mighty waters, who brings forth chariot and horse,
> army and warrior; they lie down, they cannot rise, they
> are extinguished, quenched like a wick: "Remember not
> the former things, nor consider the things of old. Behold,
> I am doing a new thing; now it springs forth, do you not
> perceive it? I will make a way in the wilderness and rivers
> in the desert."

So then, here is the short answer to our question—God is at work in our circumstances even when His handiwork is absolutely and completely invisible to us. But in our despair, we may be tempted to think, *So what? What if He is at work. I can't see it. I can't feel it. And it doesn't do me a bit of good.*

The antidote to the hopelessness in those emotions lives in God's promise in verse 19 that says, essentially: *Don't you see? I'm doing something miraculous and fresh and new. I'm the only one Who can. So trust Me.*

Remember Who I Am

As you well know, our fictional setup of a face-to-face conversation with Christ isn't likely for us this side of eternity. But I can think of at least one desperate person in eons past who did get his moment before the Almighty. That man, the godly and tortured businessman, father, and husband Job (of Old Testament fame), came armed with questions, ready to plead his case.

But God didn't answer Job directly. In fact, we don't have evidence that Job ever got to ask his questions. Instead, God spoke out of a mighty whirlwind and began questioning Job: "Who is this that darkens counsel by words without knowledge? Dress for action like a man; I will question you, and you make it known to me. Where were you when I laid the foundation of the earth? Tell me, if you have understanding" (Job 38:2–4).

A few verses later God asks, "Who has cleft a channel for the torrents of rain and a way for the thunderbolt, to bring rain on a land where no man is . . . and to make the ground sprout with grass?" (Job 38:25–27). The obvious answer? Only God has done that. Only God could do that. It's as if He were saying, *I am the Creator. I make a way. I forge a path. I control the destiny of every creature. I cause fresh water to spring up in wastelands.*

Significantly, we hear this reminder first in answer to our questions of deepest desperation. Shall we give up hope? Not for a millisecond, if our hope is placed in the Mighty One Who displays His power in all He has done.

Forget Your Past

After the call for us to remember Who He is and what He does, God tells us: *Don't look back, look forward to something new* (paraphrase of Isa. 43:19). That's odd. He'd just told them to remember. Now He says to forget?

Yes, that's what we need to do—forget the plans we had made, forget the hopes and dreams we'd held, forget the path we'd been trying to plot with our own GPS.

People without faith planted in God will hang on to their own purposes. It was people like this who made the blasphemous statement recorded by the psalmist: "They spoke against God, saying, 'Can God spread a table in the wilderness?'" (Ps. 78:19).

Well, *can He? does He?* Yes, and yes. Yet, depending on God will seem a cop-out from the perspective of one who doesn't know His creative genius. In fact, in good fiction of our day, it would never be done. It's called *deus ex machina*.

In case you're not familiar with the term, here's a definition from answers.com:

> (1) In Greek and Roman drama, a god lowered by stage machinery to resolve a plot or extricate the protagonist from a difficult situation.

(2) An unexpected, artificial, or improbable character, device, or event introduced suddenly in a work of fiction or drama to resolve a situation or untangle a plot.[1]

A novelist who wants to be published in today's market cannot resort to this plot device. If she does, she'll be laughed right out of the bookstore.

And yet our God, the only true God, invites His people to "behold" the new thing He is creating before our eyes. *Deus ex machina.* God is intervening in our circumstances—not lowered in by stage machinery, but coming down of His own accord to become intimately involved in creating a path through the desert wasteland. A path where we know for sure there could be no way.

Adjust Your Lenses

He's incredulous that we aren't able to see His path. So why can't we? Is it because we're looking backward for something else, something known, something wanted? Is it because we're looking for our help to come from more conventional means? Is it because our eyes are too out of focus to see what He has placed right before us?

He's practically shouting, *Look! Don't you see it? Won't you perceive what is right before you?*

I can't tell you the number of hours I've logged recently in our ophthalmologist's office. Like Mom before him, Dad just learned that the lenses he was born with have become fogged—clouded and soon-to-be useless. The only solution (other than allowing it to continue until he goes blind) is to have the old lenses destroyed and replaced by synthetic lenses—cataract surgery.

He can choose, in his surgery, to have his astigmatism corrected with his new lenses. This can help him focus to a sharper point than he's ever been able to achieve unaided by glasses. In this way, the replacement lenses will be even better than the ones he was born with.

Still he's leery of the procedure. He told the surgeon he really wants the "factory equipment" . . . nothing newfangled. But now that he's been talked into the surgery complete with astigmatism correction (boy did his doctors, Mom, and I have to do some serious talking!), his eyes will see through the new lenses lots of new things. He'll focus better than he ever did.

Like Dad, maybe it's time for us to have our lenses adjusted. Maybe that's what God is inviting us to do—to get rid of the fog and astigmatism that is keeping us from focusing on what He's doing right in front of us—on our behalf.

In Isaiah 43:8, God makes an invitation to "people who are blind, yet have eyes, who are deaf, yet have ears!" He invites them to come and see what He is doing—He calls them (v. 10) His witnesses.

I suspect in their focus on one issue, Cam and his wife missed everything else God was at work doing in their lives. All the blessings they did have from Him. All the promise and potential they received from His hands. They were people blind with eyes, deaf with ears.

That's why I imagined that Cam's wife initially would respond to Christ by feeling ashamed: "You'll think I don't appreciate everything You've given me."

Now, let's not be too hard on her. Any one of us who is trying to do life God's way, to serve Him faithfully, to accomplish His plans might still be tempted to focus on what she hasn't than on what she has. But in focusing eye to eye on God, we would begin to understand that we've been looking for His intervention in all the wrong places.

Check Your Expectations

The "new thing" God told us He was busy accomplishing isn't likely to be anything we'd expect, but it certainly will be great and mighty—simply because it's His creation. It's a theme repeated often in Isaiah:

- Behold, the former things have come to pass, and new things I now declare; before they spring forth I tell you of them. (42:9)

- Then shall your light break forth like the dawn, and your healing shall spring up speedily; your righteousness shall go before you; the glory of the LORD shall be your rear guard. (58:8)

So, if our eyes are focused on Him, then we'll begin to make out the new things He's promising—good things.

I know of a congregation of believers who prayed for years that they would have a permanent place of worship. For years, they scrimped and saved. For years, they leased one building after another. For years, their best efforts were foiled at every turn. At least some of the worshippers had given up believing that the answer would come at all.

Then, in what amounted to a split second, they received a tip that a church building was available—at a price that was, frankly, unbelievably low. And within weeks, they found themselves occupying the property as owners.

I chatted with one of the members last evening, and her comment was, "Even all these months later, we're all reeling at the way this happened. We'd waited and waited. But once it got going, it was so quick."

I suspect that's what Isaiah 58:8 is all about. Once it starts, fasten your seatbelts. Your waiting will be over, and, like the sunrise, God's provision will burst onto the scene with amazing quickness. *Deus ex machina*. God at work—not a copout, but a marvelous reality.

Now, Back to the Studio . . .

The Guest draws Cam and his wife into a three-way hug—His strong arms bolstering them as if encouragement could be transferred by skin-to-skin contact.

Now, that was an honest question, beloved. You are right in bringing it to Me. The issue is, though, that you may feel My answer is incomplete. Because, if you are asking whether or how you will become parents—that is something I will not tell you just now.

Can't You please . . . ?

If we could only know . . .

I will not answer that today. But if you are asking whether you can continue to trust Me to be at work on your behalf, always with your best interests at heart—that is an answer I will give you.

That's something, I guess. Right, Cam?

Uh. Huh.

I will offer you the same promise I gave the prophet Isaiah to encourage the people in his day who were like you—those who had stayed faithful to Me but were afraid I had chosen not to act on their behalf. Hear this: I specialize in making a way where there seems to be no way. I do not want you to live in the past filled with what-ifs. Those children you did not get to adopt found the homes My Father had ordained for them. Do not wallow there. Look ahead to the new thing I am doing on your behalf. You do not see it yet, but I do. Keep looking—focus your attention and efforts on finding My Father's purpose for you today, and each today that follows. And soon you'll see Him doing something special and new on your behalf. You will see it in due time.

So there's hope?

Yes, My beloved ones, there is great reason for hope.

Discussion Questions

1. God opens His comments to Isaiah with a reminder of Who He is and what He has done for Isaiah and His people. When

you feel most disappointed, which aspects of God's character lift your spirits? Why is it helpful to recall them?

2. In the chapter, we read of Job and the way God responded to his questions. Read Job 38:2–4, 25–27. Why didn't God answer directly? In what ways was His answer better than Job expected? Consider this thought: What if the privilege of this encounter with God were the *real* reason Job had to come to this moment of desperation?

3. If you're to be satisfied with God's answers, what baggage from your past will you need to "forget"? What will it take for you to be willing to do that?

Chapter 8

When I'm Exhausted, Do You Care?

As the Guest's conversation with Cam and his wife winds down, the studio comes awake. The Reporter settles in, checks with the control room, and motions for Him to return to the set. Cam's wife leaves the studio refreshed enough to return to her work at the pregnancy center.

Our first interview this afternoon is with a mom who asks to be called Frazzled in Freeport. Sir, are You ready for her? From what the crew reports on location, this might be a bit chaotic.

I am ready. It may be good for all of us to drink in a little youthful energy from Frazzled's family.

If You say so! Here we go. Frazzled in Freeport, are you there?

Just got things settled down here. Thanks for doing this after lunch.

Our pleasure.

Hello Frazzled. I am so glad to talk with you again. It has been a while.

The Location Camera Operator is feverishly attempting to keep Frazzled centered in frame. As she talks—and presumably listens through her monitor—she is in constant motion: reaching to retrieve stray toys, stack lunch dishes, keep sippy cups from tumbling, and redirect two preschoolers away from the camera's eye.

Yes, well, it's hard to get a minute, You know? Even now. It's nap time for my youngest—that's why this is our best chance to grab a minute. I set the twins up with some games since they refuse to nap. Mom is watching her talk show. I hope the volume isn't messing with your audio. Well, she should be okay for now—she has a glass of ice water, her TV remote, and a magazine, that should do for. . . . I'm babbling, aren't I? Sorry 'bout that.

No worries, Daughter. I am not offended.

Good. I mean, I'm glad to know that. 'Cause sometimes it feels like, well, You're mad at me. Like that's why You put me in this life that feels like I'm spinning in a Tilt-o-Whirl and no one is at the controls to shut it off.

The Reporter feels her journalistic urge to rephrase a statement and clarify, so she jumps in with . . .

So you feel like your life is an amusement park ride gone haywire?

Yeah. Especially the haywire part. Things weren't crazy enough with twin toddlers, but then the baby came along. Next my mother-in-law's broken hip left her unable to help herself, so we moved her hospital bed into my family room. There just isn't any end. Most days, if I had time to think about the 1001 things I have to do, I'd just want to cry. Except I'm too tired to think or even to cry.

We can see that . . .

A preschooler plants herself between her mother and the camera. She grins infectiously. The camera's ambient mike picks up her voice rather loudly. The Guest grins just as infectiously.

Hi!

Well hello, Little One.

I wanna see You too! I learn about You in Sunday school.

Frazzled finally succeeds in pushing the child back. But the Guest holds up His hand to stop her.

I am interested in what Little One has to say. Please do not send her away. Child, tell Me what you learned in Sunday school.

Um that You are nice and You love me and You have room on Your lap for little kids.

Yes, all that is true.

I like those stories my teacher tells.

I am glad. You keep listening to your teacher, okay?

'kay.

Is there something else on your heart, Little One?

Yep. Can you tell my mama to come and play with me? My brother won't share his toys, and I don't like to play with him anyway. He's mean. And he calls my games baby games. But Mama could come and play dress-up with me—that would be so fun!

I tell you what. If you let Me talk with your Mama right now, I will see what I can do about getting you a playmate later.

'kay! 'bye!

You want me to play *dress-up*? Really? Weren't You listening? I'm beat. I don't have a spare millisecond. Everyone wants a piece of me. They all need me. I don't even *know* what I need anymore. I'd settle for a bubble bath that doesn't get interrupted by someone looking for her lost blankee or tattling on his sister or needing her pillows fluffed. Don't You see all the demands on me? Don't You know I'm ready to collapse? Don't You even care?

W hether or not we are or ever will be parents, we all have felt as emotionally drained and utterly overwhelmed as our friend Frazzled in Freeport is feeling. And she voices a universally relevant question that at one season or another has been on every one of our lips. Even the twelve disciples voiced it one dark and stormy night: "Jesus, don't You care? We're drowning!" (paraphrased from Mark 4:38).

One of the main thrusts of my writing ministry in recent years has been to caregivers of aging parents—and no one knows the drowning feeling better than this group of self-givers. Because of my book, *The Overwhelmed Woman's Guide to . . . Caring for Aging Parents,* women visit and post on my Facebook pages, blog, and website about their challenges in doing what Frazzled described—giving themselves away by caring for their loved ones while trying to salvage what's left of personal life and health.

The biggest issue for caregivers seems to be carving out time to care for their own physical and spiritual health. I know. Because I spend many hours each week as a caregiver for my dad. So, I can attest to this: a wrung-out caregiver, like a wrung-out mom, is little good to anyone. Overwhelmed. Drowning. Frazzled by life gone haywire. As the *Woman's Study Bible* puts it, "Fatigue can make a 'nag' of anyone! Nothing goes further to make a woman less able to cope with unruly children, household or job crises, and thousands of other mundane irritations."[1]

Frazzled's complaint takes a slightly different form in Isaiah's writing. Apparently the people, seeing disaster looming, were desperately misguided and disillusioned. So, they assumed, "My way is hidden from the LORD, and my right is disregarded by my God" (Isa. 40:27). The prophet knew better—and told them so.

But what would Jesus say to Frazzled or to any of us who thinks God is oblivious to our exhaustion?

Remember Me?

Listen to what follows the people's complaint in Isaiah:

> Why do you say, O Jacob,
> and speak, O Israel,
> "My way is hidden from the LORD,
> and my right is disregarded by my God"?
> Have you not known? Have you not heard?
> The LORD is the everlasting God,
> the Creator of the ends of the earth.
> He does not faint or grow weary;
> his understanding is unsearchable.
> He gives power to the faint,
> and to him who has no might he increases strength.
> Even youths shall faint and be weary,
> and young men shall fall exhausted;
> but they who wait for the LORD shall renew their strength;
> they shall mount up with wings like eagles;
> they shall run and not be weary;
> they shall walk and not faint. (Isa. 40:27–31)

It seems we've been at this starting point together before. This may seem a cop-out to many who don't know God, but, to those intimately acquainted with Him the answer to all our deepest questions begins with Him—knowing Him, remembering Him, recalling His character, reflecting on His attributes. So that's where the prophet takes us:

How can you think for a moment that God doesn't know where you are or what circumstances threaten to overwhelm you? Don't you know Who He is? He's the Creator of "the ends of the earth." He's not tired or inattentive. His ability to infuse you with strength is endless. His willingness to give you every ounce of energy that you need is boundless.

Pie in the sky? I don't think so.

Then why when we get in so deep do we think He's letting our Tilt-o-Whirl spin out of control? Maybe because when we're exhausted and we're trimming everything but the most crucial items from our agendas, our devotional time with Christ seldom makes it past the first round of cuts. In scheduling Him out, we too easily forget all about His provision and resources.

The Nelson Study Bible notes that in Isaiah 40:27, the people aren't questioning "God's omniscience, but His good will."[2] In other words, they knew He *could* help, but they didn't think He *would*.

I've been there—recently, as a matter of fact.

I can't remember having one bit of an issue with the awesome power and majesty of God. When I was younger than our story's Little One, I'd learned lyrics to a ditty drawn from Psalm 50:10: "He owns the cattle on a thousand hills, the wealth in every mine." I knew He had the provisions I needed desperately. But somewhere I lost hope that He would pour them into me.

My problem was that in not wanting to presume upon Him, I was no longer expecting Him to act on my behalf. It's a hopeless feeling and an exhausting one.

The first remedy was to remember His character—His love, His kindness, His graciousness. And sometimes, like in our story, that reminder comes out of the mouth of not prophets, but babes. That's why I put this truth in the mouth of Little One in the drama, "I've learned that You are nice and You love me and You have room on Your lap for little kids." It's simple. But its clear truth makes all the difference.

Adjust Your Expectations

Okay. We get it. God knows and cares. He can and eventually will bring us through this season. Our job in the interim is to remember Him by carving out time to remind ourselves of His tender loving care.

But can He help us cope with our exhausting reality—all the days, months, or even years before the season finally changes and the overwhelming expectations wane?

Part of our answer comes from Isaiah 40:31, which talks about running without weariness and walking long distances without fainting. We might want to board a transport vehicle to get us to our destinations without any effort on our part, but that's not how God suggests we arrive. He calls on us to do something: to run or to walk. He calls on us to do this, not assuming we have the resources, but rather by tapping into strength and energies only He can offer.

God never promised us a life spent perched on down-stuffed pillows while a servant fans us with ostrich-feather plumes and feeds us peeled grapes. That wasn't even life in Eden. Remember in that perfect garden, God gave Adam and Eve the task of tending the garden. True, there were no weeds or thistles, but there was healthy work.

So, looking for a shortcut out of hard work isn't God's plan. He didn't sign us up for boredom or inactivity. Instead of looking at our work as an imposition on our me-time, what if we viewed it as an act of service toward God? I created Frazzled—her attitude and situation—to highlight our buried feelings of being imposed upon by life and everyone in it. I made her more than a little whiny because (as I've already confessed) that's how I tend to get when I'm overtired.

Ask any empty-nester; she'll tell you she realized too late that time with her tots was too short. My mom and I were talking about this as I was arranging my favorite childhood toys (practically antiques, now!) for display in my guest room. As she handed me each one, she reminisced about seeing my tiny hands play with them. Finally she blurted out, "I wish I'd taken time to sit on the floor with you and play. Barbie dolls. Dress up. Lincoln Logs. Grocery store. Whatever. But I was too busy then. I wish . . ."

So what if toys litter the family room? So what if dinner comes out of a bucket rather than a gourmet cookbook? And will the world end if guests find dust bunnies under the beds? (serves them right for looking!) The mom who invests her time in her kids, like the caregiver who treasures her aging parent, will never be sorry. It's all about adjusting our expectations.

Share the Burden

Another change in perspective God might prescribe is that everything doesn't always depend on us. Sometimes allowing others to participate (while not shirking our responsibilities) is a great choice.

A woman we called "Olivia" in my caregiving book shared this story:

> Initially when my mom moved in, my brothers assumed I would take care of everything. . . . I found myself resenting that. I was getting exhausted with the details of taking care of her. It was more than I had anticipated. I had to give up my social life. I cut back on involvement at church. I was getting run down with no place to go and get filled back up again.
>
> I was being kind of a martyr—thinking I had to do it all without any help. But at the time I saw it as my responsibility alone.
>
> I finally came to the point where I either needed to ask for help or drop.[3]

In the end, Olivia's brothers responded to her plea for help, and they had the privilege of participating in their mother's care.

What about Frazzled? Would this work for her?

She's quick to assume that, when the Guest promises to find a play-mate for Little One, He is making another demand on her. But what if He means for her to ask her recuperating mother-in-law to tell Little One a story or play a game with her? What if He's suggesting Frazzled elicit Grandma's participation so the older woman will feel wanted, needed, and useful?

The principle is sound. In sharing the responsibility, we may be helping God's purposes for others.

Focus on the Eternal

Did you notice how the passage from Isaiah 40 is different from the pro-phetic statements we used in other chapters? In this case, it's the *prophet* speaking to the people—giving them good, commonsense counsel based on what he knows to be true about God. That's wonderful, of course. But in all the wise counsel we've gotten in answer to this question so far, we have yet to hear how God might speak directly. For that, I'd like us to turn to the Gospels.

In Luke 10:40, we see the familiar scene where Martha-the-overworked has complained to Jesus about her sister Mary. "LORD, don't You care that my sister has left me to serve alone?" (HCSB). Add a couple of toddlers, a recovering older adult, and a blaring TV, and you'll see our sister Frazzled in Martha's complaint.

How does Jesus respond? He nails the real problem with His servant Martha. Her heart isn't in her service. What's motivating her instead? Jesus pinpoints it, "Martha, Martha, you are *anxious* and *troubled* about many things" (Luke 10:41, emphasis added).

She was in a royal snit—utterly worked up. Those are the implica-tions of the words Jesus chose in chiding Martha. *Sister, you're all stirred up about things that are temporary* (in this scene, arrangements for her dinner party). *Settle down and notice those things that will last forever* (in this scene, the Master's teachings).

I have no doubt He would choose those words for Frazzled and every one of us who feels her frustration and exhaustion. Focus your energies and your thoughts on those things that will transcend time and space.

What would that be for a modern woman? He would expect us to nurture relationships, certainly—with our families and with our God. He also would expect us to reflect the light of God's love into a dark world in great need and show others the way to Him through Jesus Christ.

We're worried and anxious and spending our lives on the minutiae of picking up toys and uprighting sippy cups. I have a hard time imagining that Jesus would be all that concerned with these when there's so much that is more pressing to do. Choose the better, He'd tell us. Spend your energies on what will last forever.

The Rest of the Story

There's also a gentle, comforting word Jesus certainly would use. "Come to me, all of you who are weary and carry heavy burdens, and I will give you *rest*. Take my yoke upon you. Let me teach you, because I am humble and gentle at heart, and you will find *rest* for your souls. For my yoke is easy to bear, and the burden I give you is light" (Matt. 11:28–30 NLT, emphasis added).

Rest is the key. Even Frazzled knows that's what she needs. She just doesn't know how to get there. The beauty of Jesus' promise is that He doesn't just demand that we rest, He provides a way for us to reach *rest*. He offers to teach us how to get there. Even better, He offers a burden exchange—Jesus offers to be the ultimate sharer of our burden. He exchanges our crushing one for His light one. He replaces our chaotic striving with His gentle, restful workload.

His prescription is that we do nothing more or less than come to Him and dump our loads at His feet. In that, Frazzled was right on the money.

Now Back to Our Interview . . .

Oh, my dear sister, Frazzled, you are all stirred up about so many things. You are giving yourself away in worry for the sake of the temporary. It may seem like no one is at the controls, but that is an illusion. Your loving Father in heaven is never inattentive. He does not leave the controls of your life for the tiniest moment.

He's really in charge of all this . . . this bedlam?

Is it really that bad?

I guess not.

Your little ones will grow tall and independent. Your mother-in-law will recover. In truth, these days are short. The opportunities they present to create loving family bonds have the tiniest of windows.

The two preschoolers tug on their mother's arm—her eyes reveal the struggle within.

Oh no, what *is* it now?

Frazzled, My daughter, consider this moment a treasure, not an imposition. Hold them tight, and let them feel My love through you. Everything else will have its time, but for now, choose the better. It cannot be taken away.

The camera pulls back to reveal Mom and tots snuggling close in a toy-strewn room with the drone of the TV as their soundtrack.

Discussion Questions

1. Isaiah 40:28–31 lets us know God never tires. But we do. In what areas do you need Him to replace your exhaustion with

power and increased strength? What would it look like for you to "rise up on wings like eagles"? How is it possible for you to run and not become weary?

2. In this chapter was a quote from *The Nelson Study Bible,* which says the people aren't questioning "God's omniscience, but His good will." When have you found yourself doing that? How did this affect your relationship with God? How did it affect your relationship with your loved ones or coworkers?

3. Using Jeremiah 31:20, 25, write how a mere mortal can tap into God's resources to find the strength to do the work He sets before us.

Chapter 9

Who Will
Love Me?

From the control room, the Producer announces a two-minute break in recording to change lavaliere mike batteries and recheck audio levels. She tells everyone to stay put, because she already has established the link to the next interviewee. Mikey, the Audio Recordist approaches the Guest and makes small talk as she opens the battery pack hooked to His sash. She fumbles nervously with the latch in her left hand while juggling batteries in her right.

Well, Sir, that was an active household, wasn't it?

Indeed, it was lively.

I don't know how she'll keep sane in all that chaos. I need my order—and my quiet.

I do believe Frazzled has a new perspective on dealing with the energy her children exude. Her life will be transformed. She will be able to accept and give love so much more freely.

Must be nice. I mean, I wouldn't mind having the problem of too much love in the house.

Do you not have enough love in your house?

Forget I said anything about love. I've got to get the other batteries changed and checked—you heard Boss Lady, no time for idle chitchat. You're all set.

As the Audio Recordist moves on to the Reporter's lavaliere, the Guest's eyes remain fixed on her. The Reporter notices and, before she can help herself, she says she's left something for the next interview in her office and dashes out the door. Wasting no time, the Guest catches the Audio Recordist's hand and pats the seat now vacant beside Him.

Me?

Yes, Mikey. Please sit here and explain what you meant about love. We have time right now.

I really don't want to get into it. I don't want anyone around here to know my weakness. You know, they'll attack it. Piranhas, all of them!

Everyone else has other concerns at the moment. It is just you and Me. You know you can trust Me not to exploit your weakness. You do know that, do you not?

I s'pose.

Well, then, tell Me everything.

Where to start? Um. I'm alone. Not in a relationship, You know? Of course You know, what am I saying?

And that is not of your choosing?

I definitely want to be in a committed relationship. I just can't find someone willing to commit.

And you have tried to be in a committed relationship?

Sure. Dozens of times—well, not dozens, but quite a few. Counting backward, there was Tom. He moved in for a while, but split to be with my best friend. Before him, there was Jim—no Bill, then Jim. Bill was no good from the start. He had baggage from his first and second marriages, not to mention child support to both families that he was perennially late in paying. He was always broke, so he was with me just to live in my condo and eat my food. Now Jim, he had serious potential. But we couldn't get along up close. We could be friends, but not live-ins. When I was just out of college there was Paul. We had a wedding date selected. But then he started slapping me around—a neighbor overheard, and the police got involved. When Paul got out of the lock-up, he said he didn't need all this complication. And he split, that night.

That is a long list of relationships but not much commitment in any of them.

Well, the good news is that after Tom I was so depressed—I mean he was cheating on me with my *best* friend—that I actually stepped into a church. I'd never been in one before. But it was Christmas Eve and something just drew me in. It seemed like the place to go that night. Anyway, that's where I heard the message about You for the first time in my life—that You could forgive me and make me clean. And I came to faith.

I remember that night well. The crew in my Father's studio threw quite a celebration for your homecoming.

Really? Cool. Anyway, since then, I've sworn off men! I mean, I can't go to the places I used to go to meet 'em. So, it's just safer to stay away. If only I could be satisfied the way I am, everything would be great.

But you are not satisfied alone?

Sadly, no; I'm not. When I see a household like Frazzled's—I am *so* jealous. I lied when I said I like my order and quiet. I can't even make myself believe that. I'd kill for her bedlam. Maybe not *kill*, but I'd give nearly anything to have it.

Then your question for Me flows out of these experiences?

Yeah. I want to ask You: Is there anyone out there, anyone at all, who could ever really love me, for me?

The short answer for Mikey is, yep! You're talking to Him. Your search for someone to love you unconditionally, even when you're feeling unlovable, ended the moment you came to faith in Jesus Christ—the night you sought and received His forgiveness and entered into relationship with Him as your Savior.

Listen to what the Lord said about the people He chose for Himself, "I have loved you with an everlasting love; therefore, I have continued to extend faithful love to you" (Jer. 31:3 HCSB). Older translations, quote that last phrase as "with lovingkindness have I drawn [you]" (KJV and others). It's a picture of tender God-love. It's seeking, drawing, and extending itself toward you and me.

Woven from Genesis through Revelation is the unbelievable story of God's love that seeks His beloved children and lavishes His kindness on them. Even more amazing, the apostle Paul writes, "God shows his love for us in that while we were still sinners, Christ died for us" (Rom. 5:8). We couldn't earn that perfect love, and we still can't do anything to be worthy of it. But it's there for us—waiting—before we even know enough to ask for it, before there is a shred of lovability in us.

If that's true, then why does Mikey still feel empty, still crave a love she can't reach? Why do I sometimes feel that way? Maybe you do, too, regardless of your relationship status.

I was on an airplane bound for a getaway in Hawaii last winter when I began to see why I was feeling a lot like Mikey. I was doing my devotions at thirty thousand feet when I stumbled over Psalm 91:14: "Because he holds fast to me in love, I will deliver him; I will protect him, because he knows my name." What a loving thing for God to promise—to deliver me and protect me. But that wasn't the point that struck me in that moment. It was that first phrase: "because he holds fast to me in love." (I don't get all hung up on he's and she's in Scripture—if there's a promise, I take it as mine.)

That phrase reminds me of my responsibility in this relationship with the Almighty Creator. My part (same as yours) is to hang on tightly to Him in love. To tie up all my hopes, all my passions, all my energies in loving Him. No matter what's going on in this world that would try to detach me from that secure connection with my Beloved, I must keep holding on.

The Almighty's love is the very gift we're seeking and feeling is in such short supply. But the problem isn't with the Supplier—He makes a ready supply available to each of us. No! The problem is with the receiver—with *us*. Instead of receiving, we tend to go around doing what country singer Waylon Jennings describes as: "Looking for love in all the wrong places."

Love Explained

Maybe it would help to understand what God means when He describes Himself as *love*. It's the fiber of His character. If we're to understand Him as much as our little minds can, we need to learn about this God-love that's so different from the temporary loves we experience in relationships among our peers. I like the way Psalm 136 emphasizes this difference. I think it pops the most in the HCSB translation, because it's laid out on the page as a poem.

All twenty-six verses end with the same refrain. Anything planted twenty-six times in a single poem gets my attention. What is that refrain? *"His love is eternal."* The psalmist takes us from the moment of creation through all God accomplishes for His people, and at every juncture, he reminds us that God's love is unchanging, forever, enduring, steadfast, absolutely dependable. It is *eternal*.

Listen to one series of verses that I suspect Christ would speak to Mikey and to us:

> He remembered us in our humiliation
> > *His love is eternal.*
> and rescued us from our foes.
> > *His love is eternal.* (vv. 23–24 HCSB)

He has been watching as each painful event of our lives has unfolded, and no event changed the fact that He was always loving us and always offering a way of rescue.

Understanding this love can't be easy for us. In fact, the apostle Paul prayed for this same understanding for the believers in Ephesus. It was something he longed for in their lives but knew wouldn't come without focused, intense effort:

> I fall to my knees and pray to the Father, the Creator of everything in heaven and on earth. I pray that from his glorious, unlimited resources he will empower you with inner strength through his Spirit. Then Christ will make his home in your hearts as you trust in him. *Your roots will grow down into God's love* and keep you strong. *And may you have the power to understand,* as all God's people should, how wide, how long, how high, and how deep his love is. *May you experience the love of Christ,* though it is too great to understand fully. Then *you will be made complete* with all the fullness of life and power that comes from God. (Eph. 3:14–19 NLT, emphasis added)

May you have "the power to understand" God's love, Paul prays. What does that mean? One key attribute of God's love is selflessness, which He expressed when He gave Himself away to pay the penalty we owed.

Consider the parable Jesus told about the Good Samaritan. The loving one in the story is the Samaritan who, at great cost to himself, cared for—personally, tenderly, generously—the one who could not repay him, the one who would have ignored him had the tables been turned.

Other ways Jesus explained this give-yourself-away love include praying for those who seek to harm us and giving more than we're asked when someone demands sacrifice from us (Matt. 5:39–47).

It's unnatural—that's what it is for us. But it's natural for God; love is, after all, the core of His nature. Ephesians 3:19 tells us as we experience that love, we'll get the completeness we long for, the "fullness of life and power" that only this love connection with God can provide.

Love Experienced

There's another layer of understanding here: "May you *experience* the love of Christ." It's not enough for us to have head knowledge. In our fictional example, Mikey knew with her mind that God loved her. She had accepted Christ as her Savior. She just had no idea He could be the answer to her heart's love-search. Her mind was in the game, but her heart hadn't followed.

I don't think it's a problem unique to a new believer. I fight the same battle daily. Even after more than four decades of following Christ, my heart isn't always in the game. I suppose that's true of my relationships with my family, too. Some days, I'm all in; but others, I approach by rote, by duty rather than love. Do you know what I mean?

Thankfully, God is always *all in*. Think back to Jeremiah 31:3 (KJV): "with lovingkindness have I drawn [you]." There is a consistency. The Lord continues to draw us daily with kindness. With compassion. With grace. When I'm ratty and rotten and snippy and hard as granite. When I'm so unlovable I can't stand being with myself. Still the persistent love of Christ calls me to sink the roots of my heart into the soil of His amazing, self-giving, life-impacting *love*. The love that finds me precious. The love that stays when I've succeeded in pushing every other soul away.

That's the true test of love in my mind. If it's real, I won't be able to pay for it, squelch it, or run it off by my behavior. The only love on this planet of that refined and perfect quality is God's love.

I guess there's a little bit of me in Mikey, although her life path and choices are so different from mine. Since childhood, I've made it my life's goal to dig deep into God's marvelous love and to live according to His plan for pure relationships. But in my earthbound humanness, I've still searched unsuccessfully for one man to love me—to be willing to commit exclusively and permanently to me. In that search, I've experienced the heartbreak of rejection multiple times, up close and personal.

In the decades since my two worst rejections, I've come at last to the point where, while I'd still welcome the opportunity for a husband's committed companionship, I'm learning to take comfort in God's promise in Isaiah 54:5: "For your Maker is your husband, the LORD of hosts is his name." The God Who created me loves me *that* much. And I'm learning to accept that love as the answer to my great need to be treasured by someone. Given time, someone in Mikey's situation may just come to that same realization—and so can each of us, regardless of marital status. For without Him, we are incapable of experiencing selfless love. We wouldn't even know it existed.

Love Reflected

Once we've begun to experience that love, we have a new responsibility: to respond in kind and to reflect the love of God back toward God. The apostle John couldn't make it plainer: "Anyone who does not love does not know God, because God is love" (1 John 4:8).

If that weren't enough, Christ reiterated a command from Deuteronomy: "Love the Lord your God with all your heart and with all your soul and with all your mind and with all your strength" (Mark 12:30). So, once we've found it, He expects us to take action with an all-in love. Look at the emphasis on "with all your . . ." in that quote. It's there four times—just in case we were tempted to hold anything back.

Paul offers an explicit word picture of just how we're to live that love:

> Love is patient and kind; love does not envy or boast; it is
> not arrogant or rude. It does not insist on its own way; it
> is not irritable or resentful; it does not rejoice at wrong-
> doing, but rejoices with the truth. Love bears all things,

believes all things, hopes all things, endures all things. (1
Cor. 13:4–7)

That's the kind of trusting, faithful love we're invited to show Him.

Jesus put it succinctly: "If you love me, you will keep my commandments" (John 14:15). Which ones did He mean? I'm glad you asked.
Others have wondered that, too. One guy asked Jesus pretty much that
same question when he wanted to know which commandments were the
most important. Jesus' answer came just after the instruction that our
greatest need is to love God fully. Once we've done that, Jesus says we're
to: "love your neighbor as yourself" (Mark 12:31).

The outcome of loving God with all our hearts will be that we love
those He loves—our neighbors, our families, our friends, even our enemies. Again, listen to John's explanation: "No one has ever seen God; if
we love one another, God abides in us and his love is perfected in us" (1
John 4:12).

So, rather than seeking someone to love us, we who love God will
make the first move and love others with all our hearts. I love the way
author Anne Graham Lotz puts it, "The first secret to loving others is
to immerse yourself in a love relationship with God the Father, God the
Son, and God the Holy Spirit."[1]

I wonder, then, whether a better question from us toward our Lord
would be to turn Mikey's question upside down: *Lord, is there someone I
can love with the kind of love You've shown to me?*

Now Back to the Newsroom . . .

Mikey, My sweet child. You are coming to know Me more every
day. To know how deeply *I* love you. To know how much I gave
up for you—because of My love for you. I am the love you

seek. No one could love you in a more complete or fulfilling way than I already do.

You, Lord?

Oh, yes. I have loved you for eternity past—and through eternity future. My love drew you into the church that Christmas Eve. My love reached all the way into your lonely, grieving, frightened heart to give you new life in that moment. My love celebrated the warming of your heart and your decision to accept My offer.

You love *me,* Lord?

I love *you,* Mikey. And My love for you will never fail. But I have two questions for you.

You do?

Yes, Mikey child, will you choose to love Me back—not for what I can do for you, but simply because of Who I am? And will you choose to love others as I have loved you?

Discussion Questions

1. Make a list of the times you've seen God express His love toward you. Be as comprehensive as possible. Then, post that list someplace where you'll find it the next time you're feeling unloved or unlovable.

2. Read Ephesians 3:14–19. What can you do to make your spiritual roots go more deeply into the soil of God's love? How will you act on what you discover?

3. What can you learn from the parable of the Good Samaritan (Luke 10:30–37) to equip you to love people in your life who are desperate to experience unconditional love?

Chapter 10

Who Will Comfort Me When I'm Down?

After the most recent delay, the Producer is more out of sorts than usual.
She snipes at the control-room crew and yells through the Reporter's ear-
piece for her to get a move on it.

We've got a whiney one on the line next. Keep it short with her.
I've been listening to her grumble and complain since you went
running out of here.

Sorry.

You oughta be. Anyone who asks to be called Ailing in Albany
is a loser, for sure. I don't even know her. Why should I care
about every sad and sorry detail of her most recent Lupus flare?
Get this over with. I've had enough of her already.

Is Ailing standing by?

Yeah. You've got her now. Everyone just do your job. I'll be back
when this one is over. I'm outta here.

Ailing in Albany? You're live with our Special Guest. .

Thanks, I guess.

Hello Ailing. It is good to see you looking so well.

Looking *well?* Are You kidding me? I haven't been well in years. I haven't been without joint pain in I-can't-remember-how-long. And this most recent flare has been going on for six weeks. If You can't see all my pain, then maybe You're just not the high and mighty one You claim to be.

The Reporter studies the Guest closely as He watches Ailing through the studio monitor. She expects anger at this impertinent outburst. Instead, she sees something unexpected—sadness, no, more than that, deep sorrow. And she sees restraint. For, rather than reacting, He remains silent. When she can't stand the silence another millisecond, the Reporter jumps into the conversation.

Now Ailing, that was a rather uncalled-for outburst. Our Guest has made time to be with you and to listen to you. The least you can do is to treat Him with the same respect you'd have us use toward you.

No, daughter, it is fine for this child of Mine to vent her emotions with Me. I am more than able to handle them. Ailing, I appreciate that you feel free to be so honest with Me. I do not take lightly your pain or your sorrow at having to endure this debilitating disease.

Well, that's more like it. *Looking well, indeed.*

I perceive that you are frustrated with people who assume you are as healthy as you appear to be.

Yeah. For sure. Slap on a little makeup and comb my hair, and no one believes I'm really sick. I am, You know!

Yes, I do know.

Okay, then. I wanted to talk with You because I've been feeling something else lately. Sad. I mean I'm always a little down when a flare comes on. But this is different. Sometimes I don't even think it's worth the effort to lift my head off the pillow. And no one—I do mean no one—understands. Everyone says to just buck up, stop complaining, or to pop a pill so it'll all be better.

None of that works, does it?

No. It just makes me *mad!*

I can see that.

Well, I sure don't need that coming from You, too!

I will never tell you to buck up or to stop complaining.

No. Usually You just don't say anything at all. I cry and I pray and I cry out to You again. And nothing. It's like You don't give a rip about the pain that's crushing me.

When you cry out to Me, do you wait to hear My answer? Do you search My Word to see what I am saying to you?

Well . . . um . . .

You can see and hear Me now. If you promise to listen to My answer, I invite you to bring your question to Me again, right now. I will answer, and I believe everyone on the crew could benefit from My answer, as well.

Whatever. They can do whatever they want. But as for me, I need relief, and You're the only one who could give it. I get it that You don't always do the healing thing for everyone. But isn't there someplace where I can get a little compassion and a little comfort?

Three years ago, after suffering for more than a decade, I finally had to admit that I could no longer ignore my family doctor's increasingly strong *suggestions* that I consult a specialist. So, off I trotted one snowy day in December, referral in hand. One test early on indicated that the first concern was the "C" word (cancer). That made for a terrific Christmas season for our family. A second, more invasive test determined that while cancer was pretty much ruled out, major surgery was mandatory.

So, on another snowy morning, December 26 to be exact, my folks saw me wheeled into surgery. The weather was so bad that a pastor friend of our family's couldn't even make it to the hospital to pray with me or sit with my folks—and somehow that seemed to fit my decaying mood just fine. While the surgery was a success (please don't ask to see my picture-perfect scar), something else must have been removed along with multiple clusters of tumors and benign growths: my previously solid faith in God's goodness. If you'd asked me, during the many months of my recovery, to reply to the phrase: "God is good, all the time," I don't think I could have formed the words of the expected response, "All the time, God is good."

You may have felt, as our friend Ailing has, that very angst. If you have been there, like I have, you may not have resolved to your satisfaction this issue of whether God is really as good as you've been led to believe. No wonder she (and I) couldn't find any comfort that would suffice.

I'm not a doctor, a psychologist, or a chaplain, but even a lowly patient can make an educated observation. Mine is this: there's something abrasive about prolonged illness. Like my dad's power sander, it strips emotions bare and grinds away at faith until it obscures everything we once knew to be true about God—His love, His compassion, and the assurance that He treasures us. Heading into the doctor's office, we may hold rock-solid faith in God. But give us a measure of pain, offer a frightening diagnosis (even the suggestion of one), wheel us into a lily-white surgical suite (I can still feel that ice-cold gurney), and our faith often fails the test. At least mine did.

What Is Good?

Have you ever stopped long enough to be amazed at the way the mind works? Even during those slippery slides into dark thoughts (perhaps especially then), certain memories seem to surface—a lyric, a verse, a favorite quote. I suspect this is true especially for Christ-followers, since we're infused with the Holy Spirit and one of His functions is to remind us of God's unchanging truth.

At one point in my grief, He called to my mind a book project I'd done earlier in my career. A publisher had contracted with me to create a beautiful gift volume using quotes and key themes from Hannah Whitall Smith's classic book, *The God of All Comfort*. Smith's short book is a study on the title phrase from 2 Corinthians 1:3, a Scripture I'd even used as part of my grandmother's funeral sermon a year earlier.

Upon rereading that book, I realized one passage, in particular, addresses my exact question: *Does my pain mean God is no longer good?* Smith answers decisively, yet compassionately, "We may be in trouble and darkness, and may feel as if we were cast off and forsaken [how did she know?], but our feelings have nothing to do with the facts, and the fact is that God is good."[1]

How could she say that? And how could you and I believe it, despite our feelings to the contrary? The short answer is that feelings are not reliable. They fool us all the time. So we can't bank on them.

But more than that, I suppose to emerge from our disappointment with God, we need to revisit our definition of *good*. For, if I consider God's goodness on me-centered scales, then I would expect my blessings to outweigh my sorrows. From this perspective, God's goodness would have to diminish whenever my sorrows tip the scale. What do you think about that? Is God's goodness dependent on how many good things He gives me to counterbalance the bad?

We know Smith's answer. But what does God say about how good He is? Jesus tells one inquirer, "No one is good except God alone" (Mark 10:18). So, His nature defines the concept of good. We wouldn't even be able to recognize good without Him.

God also addresses this from His own mouth in Isaiah 57:15: "I dwell in the high and holy place, and also with him who is of a contrite and lowly spirit, to revive the spirit of the lowly, and to revive the heart of the contrite."

Notice that the ones He promises here to restore and revive are those who are *contrite* and *lowly* (could anything be good-er than that?). Those humbled by pain, crushed in spirit. Those who can barely breathe because of the grinding stone that's pulverizing their hearts into dust.

In His goodness He rarely chooses to keep us insulated from pain. Think of poor Job who lost family, wealth, personal health, standing in the community, even the respect of his wife and friends.

Yet God never ceased to be good.

Think of the apostle Paul who three times "pleaded with the Lord" to remove his physical tormentor (2 Cor. 12:8). God refused the request, yet He was still good.

Think of king-in-waiting David, who lived in caves, hiding from Saul, who was seeking his life. Yet it's David who is able to make this statement of absolute faith: "Surely *your goodness* and unfailing love will pursue me all the days of my life" (Ps. 23:6 NLT, emphasis added).

Don't you love that picture of God's goodness pursuing us? I find great comfort in that word picture. But there is more. Much more.

A Heart Comforted, A Spirit Revived

While He chooses not to stop all pain before it assaults us, God does express unwavering goodness when He makes the promise we can take as our own: "As one whom his mother comforts, so I will comfort you" (Isa. 66:13).

When trying to dissect the easily tossed around idea of comfort, I went online to yourdictionary.com, which bills itself as "the dictionary you can understand." There I found this simplistic definition that gives us a few more practical word pictures:

> Comfort means to give a sense of peace to someone. (verb)
> An example of comfort is giving a sad friend a big hug.

Comfort is relief and encouragement or is a person who provides this for another. (noun)[2]

So, as a verb, comfort is a coming alongside; it is soothing; it is a heart-to-heart connection that reminds us we are ultimately at peace with our Lord.

Then there's that second definition, the noun. True comfort is a Person. In Christian terms, it is the Holy Spirit Whom Jesus introduces to us as *The Comforter* Who will come alongside us. He does more than remind us of truth. He is the arms of God wrapped around us in our hours of greatest pain.

The other day I was reading devotionally from Mark 1, and a juxtaposition of scenes struck me. What I saw in verses 10–13 was Mark's stark journalistic delivery of two events in quick succession: Jesus' baptism, where the Spirit descended upon Him visibly like a dove; and Jesus' temptation, where the Spirit drove Him into the wilderness to endure the enemy's buffeting. The significance here was suddenly so obvious that I was ashamed I'd never realized it before. The Holy Spirit is present not only as Jesus receives glory from His Father but at least as much in the next scene. The Spirit is as equally present and as powerfully active in initiating Jesus' time of unthinkable trial in the wilderness.

This is a key scene in Jesus' life that illustrates His understanding of our greatest temptations to fail. The writer of Hebrews puts it in perspective:

> For we do not have a high priest who is unable to sympathize with our weaknesses, but one who in every respect has been tempted as we are, yet without sin. Let us then with confidence draw near to the throne of grace, that we may receive mercy and find grace to help in time of need. (Heb. 4:15–16)

Did you catch all that? Mercy. Grace. Help. Our source of ultimate comfort is at the throne of grace. It's significant that the Spirit Who is our Comforter is beside Jesus in those moments. Our two heavenly Intercessors within the Godhead sympathize completely with our weaknesses. They are intimately familiar with the way pain wears on our veneer of faith. They stand with us, ready to provide the power to hang on through these darkest hours.

That power, God's power, imparts substance to the comfort He offers. Remember the apostle Paul's tormentor? God answered his plea with a statement that can revolutionize our understanding of God's goodness: "Three times I pleaded with the Lord about this, that it should leave me. But he said to me, 'My grace is sufficient for you, for my power is made perfect in weakness.' Therefore I will boast all the more gladly of my weaknesses, so that the power of Christ may rest upon me" (2 Cor. 12:8–9).

The most complete comfort God could and would offer His servant was supernatural *power*. God would use Paul's pain as a showcase for His power. He would receive glory from Paul's dependence on Him. We'd think He'd want the glory from keeping us from pain. Instead, He chooses to receive glory from demonstrating His powerful faithfulness *in* our pain.

Paul gained from the Lord's answer a perspective on his weaknesses that was healthy—in verse 9 and following he boldly proclaims that he's thrilled to be useful to God and to acknowledge his dependence on God.

What a Difference!

Let's look back at the passage from Isaiah 57. What exactly does God promise to the one who is crouched down and pulverized—crushed in spirit and discouraged nearly beyond consolation?

He promises to "revive." Twice, perhaps for emphasis, He uses the same verb: *Hōyâ*. Literally, according to language scholar William E. Vine, it means to "preserve alive."[3]

Why is it important? For one, His reviving breath of life keeps us from falling prey to despair, from being crushed by anxiety and overcome with hopelessness in our pain.

But it does more than that. Listen to the whole passage that features the title of the "God of All Comfort":

> Blessed be the God and Father of our Lord Jesus Christ, the Father of mercies and God of all comfort, who comforts us in all our affliction, *so that we may be able to comfort those who are in any affliction,* with the comfort with which we ourselves are comforted by God. For as we share abundantly in Christ's sufferings, so through Christ we share abundantly in comfort too. (2 Cor. 1:3–5, emphasis added)

Did you catch that key phrase? God's comfort in our affliction is sufficient not only to meet our needs, but for us to share with others. He enlivens us with power, because He has a job that our suffering qualifies us to do. Our receiving comfort comes with the expectation that we won't hoard it but rather share it around. In knowing His goodness, in receiving the consolation of the Holy Spirit, we'll move from self-centered to others-aware.

In this, God's power and grace are obvious. In our typical human nature, every one of us is prone to respond to affliction by cocooning, isolating, crawling into a cave to lick our wounds. So, when we, as suffering believers in Christ, come out of our caves and offer to help others find comfort, Christ uses our self-sacrifice to draw others to Himself.

I have a friend who displays this kind of self-sacrifice. Her name is Lisa Copen. When she was twenty-four, she was diagnosed with rheumatoid arthritis. Seldom free from debilitating pain, she has endured much. Instead of wallowing, she uses her pain to reach others. Here's how she tells it on her website, www.restministries.com:

One of my favorite scriptures is Psalm 119:50, "My comfort in my suffering is this: Your promise preserves my life."—He *preserves* it, *refreshes* it, *rejuvenates* it. And He wants to do the same for you, despite whatever kind of pain you are in!

I have been blessed beyond measure as I have had the opportunity to start a Christian ministry, Rest Ministries, for people who live with **any** kind of chronic illness or pain (like back pain). Did you know **nearly 1 in 2 people** in the United States have a chronic condition?

Many of our symptoms and our pain may be invisible to those around us, but they are not invisible to God. He not only sees your pain but He captures each tear as it falls.[4]

Lisa's ministry to tens of thousands of people in pain is testimony to the fact that we can use God's comfort to "comfort those who are in any affliction."

Now Back to Our Interview . . .

The Guest stretches toward the monitor with His two scarred hands—as if He could reach out and cup Ailing's quivering chin.

My sweet, precious Child, *I* am your comfort. *I* walk beside you. *I* carried your pain and bore your sorrows. *I* felt in My hands, in My feet, and in My pierced side, the pain not only of your sin, but of your disease. You feel like no one knows, no one understands. But surely you know better. You know Me better than that.

I guess I do.

I know you do. Recite for Me what you knew to be true about Me before your diagnosis.

Okay. I knew You were kind and just and loving and honest and good.

True. What else?

I knew You were sufficient and powerful enough to handle anything that would come my way.

Good. What else?

I knew You'd chosen to use me for Your purposes—that I could be a worker for You here on earth.

Exactly. Has any of that changed?

No. It's all still true.

Then take comfort in those statements that you know for a fact. As you lean on Me in your weakness, use the power I offer you to reach out to others who need comfort. You will find your comfort multiplies as you focus on others rather than brooding about your pain.

I'll try.

Good. See that you do.

Discussion Questions

1. Create your own definition of good as it relates to God. Now note how much (if any) of God's goodness depends on the situations in your life versus how much it depends on His character. If your definition of God's goodness is based solely on what He's done for you, then how might your new understanding of God's character help you redefine your idea of God's goodness?

2. How active is God's goodness in your life? How active would you like it to be? What are you going to do to change things in this area?

3. Search your Bible, your favorite devotional books, your hymnal, even this book, for quotes that tell you the truth about God: how He loves you, how He values you, what He has in store for you in heaven. Save these in a file on your computer or in a pretty notebook, and read them often as personal refreshers. Be ready to share them with others who are in need of comfort.

Chapter 11

Who Are You, Really?

Okay, gang. That's an early dinner break for you. But we have a long night ahead of us. So, get what you need and get back here pronto. You know what'll happen if you don't.

With that pronouncement and a string of expletives, the Producer bullies her way back into the studio. A young intern cowers in her wake. The Producer pushes the intern at their Guest.

This is Gen, our operator of the Chyron. She just got to the studio. She's been taking classes at art school. She has some housekeeping questions for You. Then she'll introduce You to someone else on our team who needs Your time. I presume, since You're not union, I don't need to give You a break.

As I told you earlier, I do not tire or become weary. I will be happy to talk with Gen and to Ange after her.

How did You know Ange was coming next? Oh, never mind. Talk to Gen. Talk to whomever You please. I'll be back after dinner.

But of course. Do what you must do. Hello Gen. Tell Me what I can do for you.

Yes, Sir. Thank You, Sir. I . . . uh . . .

You operate the Chyron?

Yes, um, that's industry talk for the character and graphics generator. It creates the digital graphics you see on the TV screen—like logos, graphs, charts, maps, and text. It's really cool. Would You like to see?

I would.

What used to take days to generate, especially the moving graphics, now I can do as the news is happening—some of it by just touching a screen.

You sound excited about it.

Oh, yes! I love it. 'Course in this newsroom, I'm just a cheap-labor intern, so I don't get to use all the great stuff, but it's experience to show when I go for a real job.

Impressive. You do good work, Gen.

Thank You . . . um . . . I'm sorry, I don't know how I should address You. I mean You're so important, I don't want to use Your given name—that would be awfully impertinent. But "Sir" sounds insufficient.

You are astute in your observations.

In fact, that's what I'm supposed to ask You. We always use the Chyron to generate our guests' names and credentials on screen. I'll make it look good—I'll do something special for You—have it fly in, do something classy but artistic. But I'm afraid I'm at a loss for exactly what name I should use.

At a loss? Why?

Well, You have dozens of names, and even more titles and credentials. I mean, I've been doing some reading of Your Book, and it seems like everyone and every situation calls for You to have a different name and to highlight different parts of Your job. And since I just got to the set now, I don't know which ones would be most appropriate. I haven't heard all the interviews.

I see what you mean.

If You wanted me to show all Your names, I might have to change every few seconds through the whole program. Not that I'd mind, of course, but the boss probably wouldn't like that. It could get distracting.

Yes. And that is not where we want the attention drawn.

For sure. So, You see, it's all about which aspects You want to focus on. I defer to Your choice. Whatever You want, You'll have.

Tell Me, what do the others on the set call Me?

Well, when the Producer uses Your name, it isn't in a favorable light at all. In fact, when she uses it, she isn't anywhere close to addressing You as You ought to be addressed.

I know. That hurts Me.

I'm sorry for her. I'm afraid she doesn't like You much. Lots of the others are kinda unsure. They can see that You're good and all, but beyond that they just don't know. A couple, like Cam and the Reporter, are 100 percent into You—they call You lots of regal-sounding titles like Master, Lord, and King.

How about you? What do You want to call Me?

I'm not sure I know.

Why not?

Like I said, I've been reading a lot about You. But I'd never met You before today. I wasn't even sure You existed. Now that I'm here with You, I see You're real—You're pretty down-to-earth, too. Those flaming guards over there are pretty intimidating. And they make me even more timid to ask. But Who *are* You, really?

I've never slept well in strange places, even as a teenager. I can still remember one night when our touring musical ministry group was crashing on the floor of a church rec room. After a long day of travel (our trailer had a blowout on the interstate), an evening concert, and an hour praying at the altar with kids like us who wanted to know Christ, most of the group quickly drifted off. My eyes, though, were wide open—scanning the surroundings. Then I lit on a cinder-block wall decorated by a lone poster. The backdrop was jet black. It featured nothing but text. But that was the point. Starting in magenta and moving through every shade of the rainbow until it came back to magenta, it listed in enormous print every name of Christ used in Scripture. Centered were two words in stark white: *I AM.*

Like counting imaginary sheep, trying to count the names put me to sleep before I got halfway through. The poster stayed on my mind, though. It took me three years to locate a copy to hang on my dorm wall. All those names. All those ways Jesus Christ has a direct impact on my life. Seeing them together in living color did something to me—something wonderful.

All those names made Him relevant to me as a questioning college student. He became my Wonderful Counselor when I was choosing a course of study and career path. My Prince of Peace when I was in upheaval over my dad's sudden hospitalization for heart surgery. My Advocate when I was applying to graduate schools. My Head of the Church when my pastor/grandfather died. My Word of Life when I felt called to become a journalist who uses words to express the Christ-life He places in us.

Each of His names revealed different aspects of His character to me, different ways He would meet my needs and build relationship connections with me. And best of all, He was true to each name.

That makes sense, because in the Bible every individual's name holds great significance. It reveals character. It reveals purpose, position, and authority. It reveals the essence of the man or woman. Since the Bible is

His story, His name revealed in it is most significant of all. Because He is the One Who chooses His name, in it He reveals exactly what He wants us to know about Himself and our position in relation to Him.

Our question, "Who are You, really?" finds its answer in His name. And it has everything to do with the reality of life as we know it.

Listen to the urgency and authority God used when He spoke of His name to Moses. "I appeared to Abraham, to Isaac, and to Jacob, as God Almighty, but by my name the LORD I did not make myself known to them" (Exod. 6:3). When *LORD* appears in all caps like that, it's translated from the name *YHWH*, I AM that I AM, that the Israelites considered so holy they couldn't even pronounce it. (They even spelled it without its vowels.) It was the name He gave at the moment of Moses' commissioning as leader of the slaves who would one day become His people and possess the promised land.

> Then Moses said to God, "If I come to the people of Israel and say to them, 'The God of your fathers has sent me to you,' and they ask me, 'What is his name?' what shall I say to them?" God said to Moses, "I AM WHO I AM." And he said, "Say this to the people of Israel, 'I AM has sent me to you.'" God also said to Moses, "Say this to the people of Israel, 'The LORD, the God of your fathers, the God of Abraham, the God of Isaac, and the God of Jacob, has sent me to you.' This is my name forever, and thus I am to be remembered throughout all generations." (Exod. 3:13–15)

His eternal name, I AM, is a very big deal. I love the way the psalmist puts it: "You have exalted above all things your name and your word" (Ps. 138:2). We'll look at His Word in the next chapter, but here, let's learn all we can about the Name above every name (Phil. 2:9).

What He Was Called on Earth

I Am is an odd sounding name to our ears. It speaks of One Who always was, always is, and always will be. Jesus tells the doubting people of His day, "I tell you the truth, before Abraham was even born, I Am!" (John 8:58 NLT). Startling declaration. Quite out of the ordinary—and distant from our experience or from anything in our world that can give it context.

So, He made His name more accessible to us. In the lead-up to the advent of Jesus, He supplemented I Am with a secondary name. When the people needed provision, He revealed Himself as *Jehovah-jireh* (the I Am will provide); when they were in turmoil, He was *Jehovah-shalom* (the I Am is peace); when they needed to see His great authority over the nations of the world, He was *Jehovah-tsebaoth* (the I Am of hosts).

When it came to the advent of the Son of God, when He took the form of a man, He made His name more accessible yet. The prophet Isaiah promised, "He will be named Wonderful Counselor, Mighty God, Eternal Father, Prince of Peace" (Isa. 9:6 HCSB). So practical. So needed. Counsel. Might. Eternity. Peace.

Then, He got even closer. The virgin would "call His name, 'Immanuel (which means God with us)'" (Matt. 1:23, quoting Isa. 7:14). That was more title than name. But what an amazing title it was. Almighty God, so high, so far above, so powerful, and yet so near as to be *with us*.

He had chosen for Himself one specific given name—one that many babies in that culture would also have, but one that would find its ultimate fulfillment in Him. Gabriel instructed Mary to give that name to her firstborn Son: "You shall call his name Jesus" (Luke 1:31). *Yeshua* in Hebrew. *Iēsous* in Greek. Either way, it means "Jehovah saves." Ah, the best name when it comes to meeting our need: we need saving more desperately than anything else, and so God names Himself our Savior.

Jesus is a beautiful name. But then so are Tiffany, Brittany, Cody, and Brendan. It's Who's behind the name that makes Jesus supremely beautiful.

What He Revealed about Himself

So again, we ask the question, "Who *are* You?" The people of His day asked it. "Who is this man? . . . Even the winds and waves obey him!" (Matt. 8:27 NLT).

Jesus, ever accessible to those who truly seek Him, answered in a variety of ways. I love the way John records many of these individual revelations to us in "I am" statements. While we won't be able to dig into any one of these meaningful names here, I'll give you this chart that I've created to help you explore on your own how His name indicates His power to meet your greatest needs:

You Need . . .	I AM . . .	
Provision	The Bread of Life	John 6:48, 51
Perspective	The Light of the World	John 9:5
Password to Enter His Presence	The Door	John 10:7
Protection	The Good Shepherd	John 10:11
Promise of Eternity	The Resurrection and the Life	John 11:25
Passage to Heaven	The Way, the Truth, the Life	John 14:6
Purpose	The Vine	John 15:5
Permanence	The First and the Last	Revelation 1:17
Power for Life	The Living One	Revelation 1:18

Each time in John's Gospel when Jesus revealed Himself by one of these names, the powers that be were furious. They knew that in invoking the name of I AM for Himself, Jesus was making a clear declaration of His God-ness. He was showing His deity, His uniqueness, His power and authority. And did that ever drive the rulers of that day mad! They were so obviously insufficient. But He, the Son of God, was all sufficient. In His names, He showed them up.

Let's look at those names again. This time as a seeker. As women who need God and desperately want to believe He is all we could ever need.

- You need daily bread—enough food for the day? He *is* that.
- You need to be able to see your way through the darkness of this sinful world? He *is* the Light.
- You need access to come boldly into the throne room of Almighty God to make requests? He *is* the Door—His name is the access code.
- You need protection from those who would abuse or harm you? He *is* the Good Shepherd Who lays down His life to protect and nurture His sheep.
- You need to know for sure that this life isn't all there is? He *is* the promise that there's more—a resurrection, a life beyond the grave.
- You need passage into that life so you can live today knowing you have a certain future? He *is* the Way, the Truth, and the Life. You want to approach the Father? You want to enter eternity one day? You go on the one path that leads through Him, or you don't go at all. (That absolute exclusivity, so distasteful to our culture today, wasn't my idea, but His.)
- You need to find the purpose for your life, the reason you're here? He *is* the Vine, and you are the branch—He equips all those who live in Him to bear fruit that will last forever.
- You need permanence to outlast everything that changes in your life down here. He *is* absolutely without change from eternity past through eternity future.
- You need power to overcome your greatest fears and challenges? "Fear not," He tells John in Revelation 1:17–18, "I am the first and the last and the living one . . . I have the keys of Death and Hades." Nothing could be more fearful than those two. And yet, in His death and resurrection He conquered them, locked them up, and offers us the life-giving benefits of His victory.

Why It Matters What We Call Him

Living in Jesus' day were hundreds, maybe even thousands of other *Yeshua*s. But the second name used in the New Testament with *Yeshua* designated exactly which One held all the power. And that makes all the difference—in that day and still today.

In Hebrew it was *Yeshua Ha'Mashiach,* in Greek it translated as *Iēsous Christou,* and in English, Jesus Christ—Jesus, Anointed One, promised by God through generations of prophets. Jesus Christ the One Who would save, deliver, have compassion, establish justice, rule in faithfulness, and live forever more. That's what Messiah would be. And that's Who Jesus Christ, was, is, and always will be.

It is in that name that we have the access to enter God's presence as forgiven ones, adopted and given all the rights and privileges of family. All throughout the history of the Church, we believers have prayed in the name of Jesus Christ, just as He instructed His disciples: "Whatever you ask *in my name,* this I will do, that the Father may be glorified in the Son. If you ask me anything *in my name,* I will do it" (John 14:13–14, emphasis added). And later, "In that day you will ask *in my name,* and I do not say to you that I will ask the Father on your behalf; for the Father himself loves you, because you have loved me and have believed that I came from God" (John 16:26–27, emphasis added).

It's His name that opens the door of heaven to us. The believers in Acts used this compound name, Jesus Christ, over and over. It was the name that would save (Acts 2:38), heal (Acts 3:6), transport people into God's kingdom (Acts 8:12), and liberate sufferers from the enemy's seemingly unbreakable power (Acts 16:18).

There's a huge caution, though. I'd be shuddering if I were in the Producer's shoes. "You shall not take the name of the LORD your God in vain, for the LORD will not hold him guiltless who takes his name in vain" (Exod. 20:7). Given that warning from the Ten Biggies, we'd all be wise to be judicious in how we use that name.

I empathize with Gen trying to choose just one of these miraculous names for the Special Guest. Fortunately, we don't need to choose. Take your pick. Try them out. Yнwн: *I Am* encompasses them all. Like my poster taught me back in my student days, He is all I need—in specifics and in entirety.

Likewise, Jesus Christ encompasses all He did for us at Calvary and the garden tomb when He arose in victory and took permanent charge of the keys to eternity. It's both the way He chose to be addressed on earth and the title that gains us entrance into God's forever family.

Once we take a good, long look at what He called Himself, we'll be on our way to finding the answer to our question about Who He really is.

Now, Back to the Newsroom . . .

Many have asked the question you are asking, Gen. Maybe not for the sake of a Chyron generator, but I suspect the question comes not only from your job, but from your heart.

Yes, Lord. I have been seeking You. Wondering about You. Wanting to know You.

And what have you found in your search?

Your Word makes marvelous statements about how high and glorious Your name is. How mighty and powerful. How holy and unapproachable. How absolutely self-sufficient and complete You are. Yahweh. The Great I Am.

Yes.

All that makes me shudder. It makes me frightened to approach You. But then, I see You here—right here with me—and while the power is all true, You also seem so kind, so compassionate, so approachable. Like You are here to meet my greatest need.

Yes, I am. Perhaps you would like to use the name I gave My dearest friends? To them, I was *Yeshua Ha'Mashiach,* Jesus the Christ.

Jesus Christ, my Savior. I like the sound of that.

Then that is the name you shall use. Perhaps your viewers would find it most accessible also?

Discussion Question:

1. Read Psalm 138:2. Consider and write why you believe God chose to exalt two specific things above all else, according to the psalmist: His Word and His Name. What is it about His name that makes it so important to Him?

2. What does it mean to you to have Jesus come as Immanuel, God with us? How is this unique in a world that seems to consider God to be disinterested and far away—if He even exists at all?

3. Using the "I Am" chart from this chapter, look up each time Jesus makes an "I Am" statement. Write how you've found Him true to each of those descriptions of Who He is.

Chapter 12

How Do I Know I Can Trust You?

A designer-clad woman in highline boots, black tights, and a form-fitting blazer sweeps into the studio. Her expensive perfume chokes the air out of the room as she interposes herself between Gen and the Guest. She sticks out her hand. Yet the Guest stands stone-still. From across the room, the ever-silent bodyguards touch their flaming swords; the Guest waves them off.

I'm Ange. That's pronounced with a "guh" sound. I dropped the soft "j" years ago. I like the hard "g." It fits me. As in everyone has an *angle*. Anyway, I'm the marketing and publicity veep around here. Pleased to meet Ya.

An-guh? Indeed. We have met before.

Oh, I don't think so. I've only been in the news business a short time. Came from Madison Avenue—my accounts were the highest-grossing in the business. My commercials were big time—lots of sex and lots of exposure. Anyway, the new owner wants to put this station on the map, so he's paying me to do it.

I have my hands full—trying to slick-up this place and make it an international sensation.

Why?

What da Ya mean, why?

Why must you "slick up" this place? *Why* do you feel the need to be an "international sensation"?

Are You kidding me? It's all about viewers—lots and lots of them. That sells advertisers, and that pays my sky-high contract and lines the owner's pocket. Everyone knows that. Are You from another planet?

Not another planet. But I am from another kingdom, as you know. My kingdom holds to a different set of values. You should remember that, because you rejected those values long ago.

Another kingdom, huh? Maybe we can use that angle. Could work. First, though, let's have You read this promo. Do a trial, then when Cam gets back, we'll record it for real. I'll bet a sharp guy like You could do it right in one take.

The Guest reaches for the script Ange pushes toward Him. His frown grows deeper as He reads. Finishing, He locks a furious stare on Ange. Gen backs away and even Ange looks uncomfortable, so she starts talking faster.

Yeah, I know it's over the top. That's what viewers expect. They know it's not for real. But there's just enough truth in it to entice them.

Just enough truth to entice them to do what?

We think that Your agreeing to the interview offers us a unique opportunity to get a jump on our competitors. We're going to hold the interview and run it as an hour-long news special during the next sweeps week. Sweeps isn't what it used to be, but we still do it. Year after year, we tease exaggerated stories in overblown ads to get viewers to tune in to our programming. It's expected. Everyone does it.

I am sorry, but I do not see any of that as truth.

Never mind about truth. This is bigger than that. I see a big splash on Your appearance. Drama. Intrigue. Conflict. Your story has it all. So, we're going to exploit it—to get viewers to tune in, of course. Who knows, maybe the right people will be watching and we could swing You a movie deal—a Lifetime special or Hallmark, if You prefer. Your story has been done before, but not like we'd do it. Jazz it up for today.

No! NO! Unless this script is rewritten as the whole truth and nothing but the truth, I will have no part in your promotion.

Oh *really?* You and I both know that no one will tune in to the boring truth. They want to hear the sordid, the psycho, the chilling. There has to be some way I can make You willing to help us out here. It would seem in Your best interest to get more viewers. Then they can hear Your message. You've gotta grab 'em to get 'em to tune in. You do want people to see Your story, don't You? Of course You do. You wouldn't be here otherwise. You're far too important to waste Your time on a handful of sad little viewers. We've gotta do a blitz—get the network to pay attention. Yeah, that's it! If we could hit the network—how about one of those reality shows? Think of all those viewers. I don't suppose You'd agree to do an appearance on . . .

Enough! My name and My word are My bond. When I make a claim, people can absolutely trust Me. I will do nothing to discredit the truth.

Come, now. So many people make so many claims. If I know my business—and I do—one more inflated claim won't hurt anyone. How could anyone possibly believe Your claims, or anyone else's, are take-it-to-the-bank, honest truth?

How do I know I can trust that what Christ says is true? Many ask this question, but few expect (or, I suspect, want) the answer. Given her tone (she actually surprised me as I wrote—I hadn't intended to make her seem so adversarial—so like a fallen angel), I suspect Ange's question is rhetorical. I don't guess she'd like the answer Jesus would give her.

She isn't alone. Take the old ruler Pilate, who sat in judgment of Christ and flung out a question to which he neither expected nor accepted an answer, "What *is* truth?" (John 18:38, emphasis added). Of anyone, he should have recognized *The* Truth—it was standing right there in front of him, clothed in torn-open flesh and spurting blood. Yet instead of seeking an answer, Pilate allowed the question to dangle in the din of a bloodthirsty riot.

No less than seventy-eight times the Gospel, writers record Jesus as prefacing a statement to the crowds, to the Pharisees, or to the disciples, with the Greek word *amēn*. In other places of Scripture it translates into English just like it sounds, as "amen." When Jesus uses it, though, it becomes, "truly" or "I tell you the truth," or in King James English, "verily." (In John it's always presented as the double truth: "verily, verily.") It is like Jesus is saying, *listen up with both ears. I'm telling you something that is eternally true.* And here are just a few of the follow-ups to that auspicious opening:

- "For truly, I say to you, if you have faith like a grain of mustard seed, you will say to this mountain, 'Move from here to there,' and it will move, and nothing will be impossible for you." (Matt. 17:20)
- "Truly, I say to you, whoever does not receive the kingdom of God like a child shall not enter it." (Mark 10:15)
- "Truly, I say to you, today you will be with me in Paradise." (Luke 23:43)

- "Truly, truly, I say to you, whoever believes has eternal life." (John 6:47)
- "Truly, truly, I say to you, before Abraham was, I am." (John 8:58)

The climax to all of these is in Revelation where Jesus assumes it as His name: "*The Amen,* the faithful and true witness" (Rev. 3:14, emphasis added).

These are incredible statements. Statements only God could make and keep. But can they be trusted? Can we stake our eternal lives on their verity? How can we know for sure?

I suppose the short answer is that we have a choice—to believe that *all* He says is true, or to disbelieve *all* His claims. There is no middle ground. But what if we're not sure? What if we want something or someone to believe in, but we need to see some evidence to convince us? In *Skeptics Who Demanded a Verdict,* Josh McDowell recounts the story of a prominent thinker who embarked on a real search for truth.

> Once C. S. Lewis, who counted himself an atheist, committed himself to a quest for the truth, he found that God would not leave him alone. New information kept coming to Lewis's attention so relentlessly that he felt as though he were in a great chess match in which his "Adversary" kept making "moves" that finally brought him to a point of "checkmate." The process recalls what the Apostle Paul said about the Thessalonians: "From the beginning God chose you to be saved through the sanctifying work of the Spirit and through belief in the truth."[1]

God Defines Truth

Last night, I watched a travel show before falling asleep. The host and two guests were trekking barefoot through sand dunes near Stovepipe

Wells in Death Valley National Park. The camera captures a breathtaking scene—and a telling one. Each footfall by the three trekkers shifted the amber sands. Each moment of the sun's imperceptible movement changed the colors of the sky and the shadows on the dunes. Each breath or breeze moved countless grains at will. Peaks and valleys appeared and disappeared.

Seeing this vibrantly morphing desert landscape reminded me that nothing in this world remains the same. Just when we think the ground is stable, it'll give way beneath us and take us down with it. Sport trekkers might find shifting sands playful and fun. But when one is in danger of sweltering to death in the desert of unbelief, shifting sands are downright treacherous.

Tragically for us, absolute truth has become a casualty in our cynical culture's shifting sands. Our answer to the question: *What is truth?* has become *truth is what you make it,* or *what's true for you may not be true for me.* When I was in school, they called this "situation ethics," basing it on the assumption that truth changes depending on your values, your perspectives, and what appears expedient in the moment. The teaching seemed so logical that I was nearly convinced. Nearly, but not quite.

That's because God says, "I the LORD speak the truth; I declare what is right" (Isa. 45:19), and "by Myself I have sworn; Truth has gone from My mouth, a word that will not be revoked: Every knee will bow to Me, every tongue will swear allegiance" (Isa. 45:23 HCSB).

Those absolute statements rock the caverns of postmodern thought. There is *only* one truth—but there *is absolutely* one truth. And one day everyone will (willingly or unwillingly) acknowledge it.

I love the way the *Holman Bible Dictionary* explains it: "God is the standard. God's truth (faithfulness or reliability) is the truth that is basic for all other truth."[2]

God says we wouldn't even be able to debate the concept of truth if He hadn't set the standard. Truth is what He is about. In fact, truth is one key element of Who He is. Remember Jesus' troubling statement in John 14:6: "I am . . . the truth."

So, is He? Or not?

God Epitomizes Truth

As we prepare to make our choice, let's visit the book of Hebrews, which helps us put into New Testament perspective the events and promises of Old Testament times. There the writer tells us, "For when God made a promise to Abraham, since he had no one greater by whom to swear, he swore by himself" (Heb. 6:13). Since everything in our realm of experience is subject to change, only Someone unchangeable can make and keep this promise.

That sounds like a practical application of the message God gives in Isaiah 45:23, where it's as if God were submitting Himself to some human court or question. On His own name, He swears the verity of His statement, its permanence ("a word that will not be revoked"), its application across all time and space ("every knee" and "every tongue").

Although His is the highest testimony, God's truth lines up with the experience of generations of real people. Listen to the way one called to testify, one eyewitness, puts it:

> For we did not follow cleverly devised myths when we made known to you the power and coming of our Lord Jesus Christ, but we were eyewitnesses of his majesty. For when he received honor and glory from God the Father, and the voice was borne to him by the Majestic Glory, "This is my beloved Son, with whom I am well pleased," we ourselves heard this very voice borne from heaven, for we were with him on the holy mountain. (2 Pet. 1:16–18)

Peter tells us he saw everything Jesus did in public and private throughout His ministry. Peter experienced it from a closer perspective than practically any other human. And he concludes: *I didn't make this up, folks. I heard the voice from heaven; I saw the Majestic Glory on the Mount of Transfiguration. This Man is for real, I tell you! For real!* Peter not only believed this intellectually, he put his life on the line to testify to it—and it cost him that life.

Throughout Scripture, we read one promise after another that God made and fulfilled. Sometimes it took years. Sometimes generations, centuries, or millennia. But time after time, the predictions He made, the promises He gave, came to pass despite loads of enemy opposition. Today we'd call it a "God thing."

I love the way Hebrews 11 wraps up this idea of whether God's Word can be trusted. Listed in verse after verse are dozens of characters from Old Testament days who saw God come through. Abraham. Moses. Sarah. Rahab. Gideon. Barak. Samson. Jephthah. David. Samuel. The list is hardly exhaustive. These folks were just like us. They were challenged big time. But they chose to believe. And in giving God the opening to be faithful to His Word, they proved Him absolutely trustworthy.

How do we know we can trust God? First, He tells us so. And second, the testimony of countless believers down through the centuries affirms the truth.

Find God, Find Truth

I've felt the sands shift beneath my feet. Most of us have. It could be health challenges, unexpected (or torturously lengthy) deaths of loved ones, or financial earthquakes that rock our little corners of the planet or the entire global economic landscape. I know you've been there. In those moments when I've been subject to a quaking world, I've learned to take great comfort in the assurance that God doesn't change. When He speaks, it's true. When He promises, He delivers.

Call it a crutch if you must, but I have inside me a fundamental desperation for permanence. The ever-ticking clock of eternity is built into whatever is at my core. So, I cling to the truth of God's trustworthiness.

I revel in it. And I line up with generations of fellow believers to testify to its truth.

Listen to the words God spoke in Isaiah 45:19 that leave no room for misinterpretation: "I did not speak in secret, in a land of darkness; I did not say to the offspring of Jacob, 'Seek me in vain.' I the LORD speak the truth; I declare what is right." Did you catch it? My old grammar teacher would call it a double-negative. He tells us that He didn't say we wouldn't find Him if we seek Him. Reverse the two negatives, and you find the positive promise from Deuteronomy 4:29: "You will seek the LORD your God and you will find him, if you search after him with all your heart and with all your soul." You'll find this promise repeated almost verbatim by God in Jeremiah 29:13.

I suspect this reiterated promise provides an affirmation of why as a truth seeker, C. S. Lewis found his search satisfied in trusting Christ. Even though Lewis thought he was seeking some elusive abstract concept of Truth, in his honest searching, he found that the one, true God made Himself imminently findable.

Reject Truth, Reject God

Last chapter, we considered the first portion of Psalm 138:2: "You have exalted above all things your name and your word." I promised we'd look at the second portion here. So here's my observation: along with His name, God holds in highest esteem His Word—its power and its dependability. This clarifies why I know for a fact that if Christ were ever to submit to an interview with anyone like Ange, He would never compromise. He could never be manipulated to shade the truth, to sprinkle it with even a hint of falsehood.

His name, His reputation, His promise, all these are more solid than granite and are cemented in truth.

Now, I don't mean to be picking on a particular profession. In fact, I started my career in corporate public relations. I have many dear, uncompromising friends in advertising. The setup for this fiction, though, made it easy to pick on Ange to illustrate how quickly we all can be tempted to pander to the momentarily expedient, to change our ethics depending on the situation—to make the end (getting the message out) justify the means (a little shading of the truth).

Do you see where that attempt at logic goes awry? The minute we succumb to the shady side, we lose the message. That's why most of this chapter describes the unchanging truthfulness of God's promises. If He could break one of them, the whole deal would be off.

Thankfully, as you'll recall from our earlier mention of Titus 1:2, God "cannot lie" (HCSB). So, the deal is on. All of it. Unequivocally.

And Now Back to the Studio . . .

You know, Ange, I find it odd that you feel the need to embellish My story, as if it required more drama or more out-of-this-world claims. I think I have made enough public statements that would entice your listeners to tune in.

Well, yes, but . . .

Here are a few statements I will authorize you to use in your promotion. Truly, I tell you, I am the great divider. Some would even call Me a stumbling block. Truly My claims appear foolish to those who choose to disbelieve, but they are life-giving to all who believe. Truly, I am the only way to approach God, the one and only absolute truth. Truly, I am the source of life. Truly, I am the living water. Truly, I remind you that before the ancients were born, I am.

Well, that's certainly way out there. It could work.

And Ange, there is one more thing I want to say. . . . This is for you personally, not for the broadcast—although I hold out the same promise to anyone who is listening. I am willing to offer you forgiveness for all your sin against Me, if you are willing to

acknowledge Me as the True, One and Only Son of God—the
Savior you so desperately need.

Discussion Questions

1. What do you make of God's claim in Isaiah 45:19, 23 that He
    declares and defines the truth? How can this be?

2. Given Jesus' exclusive claims in John 14:6, how would you
    explain and defend these statements to a skeptical friend,
    family member, or coworker?

3. Read what Peter wrote in 2 Peter 1:16–21. What does it mean
    to you to know that the first-generation eyewitnesses were will-
    ing to stake their lives on the truth of what they saw in Christ?
    If anything is keeping you from doing the same, what are you
    going to do about it?

Chapter 13

How Could You Forgive Me?

Throughout the interchange between the Guest and Ange, Gen takes refuge in the control room where the Reporter is beginning to log the day's recordings. When Ange struts off in a huff mumbling, "Of all the nerve, of all the nerve," the phone beside Gen rings. She picks it up, says a few words, then taps the intercom.

Master, I don't mean to disturb You, especially after that display from Ange, but there's a caller on our incoming line. She's quite insistent. She says You talked with her grandmother, uh . . . I think the name was Weeping in Westdale. She seems awfully desperate to talk with You. The Reporter offered to set her up on video chat, but she says she'd be mortified to have You see her. If only she can just hear Your voice she'd be most grateful.

Before Gen finishes speaking, the Guest appears in the control room. He picks up a second phone from the desk. Gen and the Reporter keep their heads pressed together and their ears to the receiver Gen continues to hold. The Reporter pushes a few buttons on the control board to record the conversation.

Hello.

Sir, this is Ashamed in Asheville—that's the best thing You can call me now. It's not my given name, but it's what I've become. I'm not really in the city of Asheville; I'm just heaped in ashes. Then again You know all about what I've become and just how much I have to be ashamed of. I've done so many disgusting things—there's no way You could even look at me now. I know how much You hate sin. I might as well be the picture beside *sin* in the dictionary. I shouldn't have bothered You. There's no hope for me. There's no way I deserve to hear Your voice. I've crossed the line over and over and over again. I knew what I was doing, and I kept on. I deserve the punishment I'm about to get . . . Sir, are You there? Feel free to interrupt me at any time.

I am here, and I am listening.

It's been so long since I've heard Your voice. I was afraid . . . I was sure You wouldn't take my call. But Grandma said to try You. She can be awfully insistent, You know.

Yes, she can. She has quite a grip.

I guess she really cornered You today. I've been trying to dodge her for years. But when she gets that hand around my wrist, I'm not going anywhere. I remember when I was a little girl, she used to get that grip and drag me to the platform at church. She would play the piano, and I would sing my little heart out to "Oh, How I Love Jesus." Now I look back and wonder if it was a different person in a different lifetime. I wonder if any of it was real. I remembered that scene today when I woke from my drugged haze. I have no idea where that came from—I haven't thought of it for years. It's just that suddenly I had to call her. I didn't know she was in the studio with You. I would never have interrupted You . . .

Are you calling because your grandmother made you?

No. No. I'm calling for myself. She was the one who told me You might still be willing to listen, even after all I've done. I'd been thinking about calling You for a long time, but I wanted to get cleaned up first. I've just never been able to do it. Actually, the more I tried, the worse I got.

I see.

Is there anything I can do to begin making things right—to make me worth taking back?

No.

Oh. . . . Then I guess I really shouldn't have called.

On the contrary, there is nothing you can do to make things right. But there is nothing you need to do. I am the One Who makes things right between you and My Father. All you can do is believe and ask Me to do it.

That seems too easy.

It was not easy for Me. The price I paid for you was monstrous.

I knew exactly what I was doing. How wrong it was. I knew it would hurt You. I almost felt like the more it would hurt You, the more I wanted to do it. How can I ask You to make my guilt go away? I deserve for You to make me pay and pay and pay. My grandmother says You aren't like that. That You are loving and forgiving. But how could You ever forgive *me*?

How do I entice you to read a chapter on sin and guilt? Every one of us knows all too well the faults, flaws, failures, flops, and fiascos that created the chasm between ourselves and God. Our sin is ever before us, as the Psalmist said (Ps. 51:3). It's never far from our minds. The enemy, the accuser of believers, sees to that. So, do I really want to be the one to remind you of your sin? No way! I have enough of my own—more than enough.

For that matter, we all know what our sinful hearts want to do to any messenger with bad tidings. I'm not up for that, either. I've been enjoying the friendship we've been forging, you and I, as together we've explored the deepest questions on our hearts.

Yet this most basic question, put so well by our friend Ashamed, is pivotal to our spiritual vitality. No matter how much we'd like to, we can't avoid facing it, asking it, and listening for the answer:

> How could *You*—perfect, righteous God—forgive *me*—
> chief of all sinners?

Here's the gist of the answer you'll read below. I give you the end first because I want you to stick with me. We need to come face to face with our guilt and have it dealt with once and for all, so we can benefit from this great ending. But maybe you'll go easier on the messenger if you realize I'm with you in this. Oh, and we're in some pretty esteemed company. Here's how the prolific apostle Paul, who once dared to tell Christians to follow him as he follows Christ (1 Cor. 11:1), described his own sin problem:

> Christ Jesus came into the world to give salvation to sin-
> ners, of whom I am the chief: But for this reason I was
> given mercy, so that in me, the chief of sinners, Jesus Christ
> might make clear all his mercy, as an example to those who
> in the future would have faith in him to eternal life. (1 Tim.
> 1:15–16 BBE)

We may have been the poster children for sinners, but Christ in His mercy offers to forgive us and make of us poster children of His redeeming love. That's where we'll end up. But to get to that point, where must we begin?

Let's Talk About This

The prophets in the Old Testament, under the direction of God's Spirit, never waffle on sin and its dire consequences. Neither does God when He addresses His people. We could choose from dozens of passages where He and the prophets lay it on the line. To examine our guilt, I'd like us to use a conversation God initiates in the first chapter of Isaiah. It sets the stage for all that comes after in this marvelous book of prophecy, promises, and warnings.

Let's pick up the conversation in verse 18 (although if you have time on your own, you might want to dig into the whole chapter): "Come now, let us reason together, says the LORD: though your sins are like scarlet, they shall be as white as snow; though they are red like crimson, they shall become like wool."

God calls out to the children He has "reared and brought up" (v. 2), the same ones who have rebelled against Him in the vilest of sin. To them, to us, He issues an invitation. Can't you hear God's Spirit saying this to you? *Come now, let's talk about this. You've got a problem. And it isn't going to be solved by avoiding it or denying it. How you resolve it will affect absolutely everything—your life, your death, your eternity. That's an awfully serious problem. So, I'm here. Waiting. Come near, and we'll reason it out together.*

A New Testament promise from Jesus warrants repeating as we consider whether we'll take Him up on this offer. I love it from the Bible in Basic English: "I will not send away anyone who comes to me" (John 6:37 BBE). My dad loves this verse. He quotes it often from the old King James Version, " . . . him that cometh to me I will in no wise cast out." I'm quite sure it applies to "her that cometh," too.

That's why I know Christ would certainly take Ashamed's call—and ours. If we come, if we accept His invitation to talk out our sin problem with Him, He won't turn us away. We have His explicit word on that.

The Weight of Sin

Now, let's say we've agreed to His terms. So we come. What can we expect to hear in His response? Probably not what we wish we'd hear—or what our peers and culture tell us we ought to hear. "Oh, that's all right—huggy, kissy. It's not that big a deal. It's all good. No worries."

The problem with that? Sin *is* a big deal. The biggest. It puts a wedge between God and us. No effort on our behalf can chip away one corner of the wedge. Sin is an affront against God. It's not all good—in fact, not one bit of it is good.

Old timers knew that, and it made them ashamed. That's a healthy outlook for us, too. In chapter 64 Isaiah paints a memorable, if repulsive, word picture: Sin clings to us, he says. It clothes us like filthy rags (KJV) or polluted garments. We wear it. Worst of all, its creepy, crawly, vulgar stench can't be covered by any heavenly Febreze® odor eliminator. The prophet laments, "How can we be saved if we remain in our sins? All of us have become like something unclean, and all our righteous acts are like a polluted garment" (paraphrased from vv. 5–6). Interesting, that the best he can say about the righteous things we do—not to mention the truly vile things—is that they are polluted, filthy garments.

In our story, Ashamed is wallowing in that stench. Our inclination is to do the same.

There's another option. I love the example of David—adulterer, murderer, liar. I love his example not because of what he did but because of how he responded. The prayer of his guilty heart is what we know as Psalm 51. This poem of confession holds both a right understanding of the weight of his (our?) sin and a deep faith in God's ability to solve this otherwise insoluble problem. "For I am conscious of my rebellion, and my sin is always before me. Against You—You alone—I have sinned and done this evil in Your sight. So You are right when You pass sentence; You are blameless when You judge" (vv. 3–4 HCSB).

When we approach Christ in confession—in agreement with His assessment that we have earned a death sentence by sinning grievously against Him—He's not going to stop us and say, "There, there, now." He's going to allow the confession to continue, just like He does in the interview with Ashamed in Asheville. He's going to give us the opportunity to unburden our hearts before Him. He's going to let us have our moment of realizing the gravity of what we've done. He's going to let us have a good look at the ashes that surround us.

But then comes the good news: He won't leave us there clothed in filth; He has clean, new garments waiting for us in a place of safe, restored fellowship with Him.

Forgiven

This morning as I was getting my notes together to write, I clicked open my Pandora app. When last I'd been on the station several days ago, I'd left it set on my most mellow play list. I could hardly believe the instrumental that played first up today—it couldn't have been more relevant if I'd chosen it.

First, let me remind you of a key phrase from Isaiah 1:18: " . . . though your sins are like scarlet, they shall be as white as snow." We're about to get to that second part, "white as snow." In that light, I'll tell you that the song that came up on Pandora was pianist Anthony Burger's rendition of "Jesus Paid It All." Let me share with you a few of Elvina Hall's 1865 lyrics that go with the tune Burger played:

> For nothing good have I
> Whereby Thy grace to claim.
> I'll wash my garments white
> In the blood of Calvary's Lamb.
>
> Jesus paid it all.
> All to Him I owe.
> Sin had left a crimson stain.
> He washed it white as snow.

A crimson stain, washed in blood, becomes white as snow. It's a physical impossibility. But perhaps that's why it stands out as all the more miraculous.

David's psalm has the same idea. He requests and receives soul cleansing: "Purge me with hyssop, and I shall be clean; wash me, and I shall be whiter than snow. . . . Create in me a clean heart, O God, and renew a right spirit within me. Cast me not away from your presence, and take not your Holy Spirit from me. Restore to me the joy of your salvation" (Ps. 51:7, 10–12).

What a picture of forgiveness—*joy, clean, restore, renew.* These are all words we long to have describe our hearts. They're what Ashamed thought she'd never experience again. Guilt is that way. It has us convinced that nothing ever will be right again—that we've gone one step beyond what Christ can forgive.

That's just wrong. Dead wrong. Believing it keeps us from approaching God and begging His forgiveness. Hopelessly bound in our sin. Petrified to do the only thing that can free us. Here's what the apostle John, who walked beside Jesus throughout His earthly ministry, promises: "If we confess our sins, he is faithful and just to forgive us our sins and to cleanse us from all unrighteousness" (1 John 1:9).

Our role in the drama is to confess, to own up to our sin before the only One qualified to save us from its penalty. When we do that, we are forgiven. Clean. Renewed. By Christ's shed blood, He holds out to each of us who are in Ashamed's place a new outfit (what woman do you know who doesn't drool for a new wardrobe?): the pure white robes worn by the saved ones in heaven (Rev. 7:9). Picture the most amazing bridal gown you've ever laid eyes on! That's the one He offers to you to replace your filthy rags.

Now, one more word about all this. Perhaps you've glossed over this chapter because you asked Christ for forgiveness once long ago—and you're secure in knowing your eternity is sealed with Him. Remember, though, that even believers get filthied-up by this world every day. It affects our relationship with Him and our effectiveness for Him. Remember, when John wrote, "if *we* confess *our* sins," he included himself and his already-believing readers in that "if/then" statement. Likewise, God referred to David, "a man after his [God's] own heart" (1 Sam. 13:14/Acts 13:22) *before* his fall into public sin.

So, everything we've been discussing doesn't just apply to the sinners out there in the world; it applies as much to sinners in here among our ranks.

That's why I created Ashamed as one who had once loved Christ. She is the true prodigal—*returning* to what she once knew. It isn't just the stranger whom Christ welcomes to the fold, it is His returning child whom He runs (Luke 15:20) to welcome home.

This is the time for huggy, kissy. Once Christ has applied the payment and made us clean before Him, once we're clothed in blood-washed garments, we're ushered with great flourish into the presence of our Father in heaven. Our relationship, not just our garment, is restored.

And Now Back to the Studio . . .

You ask Me how can I forgive you? My great love for you made the only possible way. My life for yours. My purity for your filth. It was exchanged in the moment when you finally came to me and asked. I have washed you clean. Though your sins stained you crimson red, I have washed you white as snow.

My Lord; my God!

Now, I do not choose to call you Ashamed. I will call you . . . Radiant.

I like that! How can I ever thank You for this feeling—this freedom?

Discussion Questions

1. Why is it that most of us hate being reminded that we're sinners? When have you felt that way? How did God overcome your resistance to confront you with the truth about your status in His eyes?

2. The key Scripture passage in the chapter comes from Isaiah 1 where God issues an invitation to His children to come and reason with Him. It sounds like the reverse of the interview setup for this book: in Isaiah 1 He does the inviting and He asks the questions. Using the passage, write what issues He might want to raise with you. Then pray your response back to Him.

3. God doesn't say, "There, there; it's okay," when dealing with our sins. Why not? Explain, so a newcomer could understand, exactly what He does instead.

Chapter 14

Why Can't I Stop Being Angry?

As the crew begins to trickle back from dinner break, the Guest stands with Gen and the Reporter near the set. The two women ask what's going to happen to the previous caller—will she recover or die? The Guest smiles knowingly as He reminds them the important thing is she'll have all her tears wiped away in heaven—whether now or later. The three look up when Cam's large frame fills the doorway. Suddenly, a force shoves the former football guard from behind and overpowers him. The women shriek and dive to the floor as a gun-wielding fiend replaces Cam in the doorway, her gun sight set on the Guest.

Blazing bodyguards, who had remained mostly out of sight, instantly flank the Guest. They unfurl formidable wings and brandish flaming, whirling swords. Two beings appear from nowhere, more fearsome than the others. In one motion they disarm and restrain the invader. While she is unable to move her limbs, the invader's eyes glower. Her mouth unleashes a high-pitched tirade of profanity, vengeance, and accusation. Unruffled, the Guest addresses the woman.

Did you wish an audience with Me?

An *audience?* You've got to be kidding. I don't have anything to say to You. I came here to make You suffer—long and miserably. Then and only then, I intend to kill You.

I am afraid that has been done, and it will not be done again.

Don't talk in riddles to me. I hate You. I hate everything You stand for. I dare You to call off your goons. The minute they relax their grip I'll . . .

May I ask why you are so driven by hate?

You tell me why I shouldn't hate You. Go ahead. Recite everything Your people have done in Your name that has stolen my innocence from me. Then, tell me why I shouldn't look forward to watching You suffer like I have.

The raging disease of anger is eating you alive, daughter.

Don't give me that *daughter* stuff. I'm not Your daughter. For that matter, I've quit being my father's daughter—he beat me over the head with that Bible of Yours. And he let others use Your authority to do unspeakable things to me. What a despicable word, *daughter.*

What would you like Me to call you?

Revenge!

I see. Let Me ask you, Revenge, where are those who have been feeding your fury?

What?

I see two women just beyond the doorway. One of them has been tossing fuel on your anger-fire for many years. The other allowed you and your weapon to pass freely into this secure studio. In fact, she suggested you come here, now, to confront Me. They have set you up for their own selfish reasons. They have no interest in seeing your anger quenched. Now, call your sister and her cohort from their hiding.

When no one moves, more flaming beings appear to snatch the Producer and Ange from their hiding places where they've been attempting to record the events using their smart phones. The beings deposit all three women at the Guest's feet, push them to their knees, and back away tentatively. The winged guards, though, continue flanking their Master. The room seems devoid of air.

I command you to speak the truth. What is your reason for victimizing this injured soul? Producer, I address you first. Why would you cause more pain for your sister?

She's only my *half*-sister. I told You about her. And if You must know: She was the pretty one. She had everything. She was the perfect example I always had to live up to. Now I have the upper hand. I like seeing her squirm. I like seeing hatred make her ugly. I like seeing her as my equal for a change.

How absolutely shameful. And you, Ange, what is your angle?

Oh, nothing so spiteful or personal, I assure You. Since You were uncooperative with my script, I figured we could get some press from recording this. A little drama goes a long way with the viewers, like I told You before.

Silence. Both of you. Revenge, what do you have to say?

I hate all of you! I'll get you for this. My own sister. And you, Ange, I know where your skeletons are buried. Don't you think I don't! And You—You knew about this and You still let them plot and scheme to destroy me?

Enough! You three succeed only in escalating distress in each other—but none of you finds a moment's peace. If you look within, you will see the great damage the cancer of anger has done to your souls. You have seen already that you are powerless to exact vengeance against Me. There is one solution, and one solution only for your malady, only one way to assuage your anger. I am willing to offer it if each of you will humbly ask Me.

The Producer and Ange scoot farther away from the Guest. But Revenge stays put. Her face contorts. Finally she speaks with a huskier voice.

If there is a way You could release me from the anger that has kept me miserable all my life, would You please do it?

Yes! Yes! That is the question I was waiting to hear.

When I was a high school sophomore, our youth choir joined the adult choir in a musical passion play. It was a huge thrill to play our parts.

It was a thrill, that is, until our rehearsals brought us to the scene in Pilate's court. The narrator read how Jesus stood before Pilate while the chief priests and elders riled up the crowd to hurricane-force fury. Instead of the narrator reading what came next, the choir became the crowd. We had to demand the unthinkable: *Crucify Him! Crucify Him! Crucify Him!* Then it got worse—as the nails pounded sinless hands onto the cross, we became the mockers: *He can't even save Himself! Let God deliver Him now!* Again and again we were to scream pitiless taunts.

My throat choked. I couldn't form the words. I'm not much of an actress, I guess.

I think the only part worse than being among the blood-thirsty crowd would have been playing the Pharisees and scribes—the ones initiating the jeers and fueling the mob's worst impulses. Jesus' earlier words against these folks must have echoed that day: " . . . whoever causes one of these little ones who believe in me to sin, it would be better for him to have a great millstone fastened around his neck and to be drowned in the depth of the sea" (Matt. 18:6). Imagine how much rage must have seethed within the Pharisees and scribes to make them positively gleeful about driving other souls to unspeakable depths of sin.

Lying in bed that night, I went over and over the scene. People literally hated the only One Who could save them from their consuming anger. They loved sin so much that their unquenchable passion was desperate to see the Redeemer suffer gruesomely. They enjoyed His anguish. They fed on it. But rather than satisfaction, their vicarious enjoyment fueled a greater thirst. It wasn't enough to see Him brutally flogged and beaten; they had to see Him crucified. Worse yet, they had to stand there and watch—and do everything in their power to multiply His agony.

Had I actually been in the crowd that day, I wonder whether I would have been one of the loudest screamers. Only Christ's saving grace mitigates our default position of being at odds with God, furious that He would dare hold us to a standard of perfection, spouting insolent threats against Him. Our director reminded us of that fact as we balked at our parts during rehearsal—*our* sin crucified Him every bit as much as the sin of the Judean mob.

Anger Seethes and Destroys

I suppose that scene gives me a greater understanding of the way anger, like that of my characters Producer, Ange, and Revenge, escalates and turns people into its puppets. Anger is unquenchable. It feeds and feeds until it has completely digested reason, common sense, and self-control. It won't stop until it has destroyed its host and everyone in its path. Then, like a virus, it seeks its next victim. Job's friend Eliphaz had at least one thing right: "Anger kills a fool, and jealousy slays the gullible" (Job 5:2 HCSB).

More helpfully, James points out not just the problem but the solution, "The anger of man does not produce the righteousness of God. Therefore put away all filthiness and rampant wickedness and receive with meekness the implanted word, which is able to save your souls" (James 1:20–21). Interesting that James is addressing not an angry mob of mockers but a cleaned-up gathering of believers.

It's easy for us to see anger in the unconverted. They can't help it. They don't have God's Holy Spirit living within them. But we can—and we do (have His Spirit)— yet, we need the reminder at least as much. Scripture repeats the same chorus from the quills of many of its writers:

> David:
> Refrain from anger, and forsake wrath!
> Fret not yourself; it tends only to evil. (Ps. 37:8)

> Solomon:
> A harsh word stirs up anger. (Prov. 15:1)
> Wrath is cruel, anger is overwhelming,
> but who can stand before jealousy? (Prov. 27:4)

> The Apostle Paul:
> Be angry and do not sin; do not let the sun go down on your anger, and give no opportunity to the devil. (Eph. 4:26–27)

> But now you must put them all away: anger, wrath, malice, slander, and obscene talk from your mouth. (Col. 3:8)

> Christ:
> But I say to you that everyone who is angry with his brother will be liable to judgment; whoever insults his brother will be liable to the council; and whoever says, "You fool!" will be liable to the hell of fire. (Matt. 5:22)

David links anger with its true source—evil. Solomon connects the awful triumvirate—cruel wrath, overwhelming anger, overpowering jealousy. Paul shows us that underlying anger is malice—fueling it is slander and foul talk. Christ says in no uncertain terms that bitter anger requires harsh and ultimate judgment.

If We All Got What We Deserve

I suspect we'd better look more closely at what Christ had to say in Matthew 5.

I'm a fairly easygoing person. Many times I succeed in being slower to anger than other people might be in the same situation. So, I tend to feel pretty good about myself . . . that is until I hear Jesus' sermon on angry words.

While "You fool!" may not be in my regular vocabulary, when I'm driving and I see some guy weaving around his lane, then I pull up beside him and find that he's texting, I'm pretty quick to yell out, "Idiot!" I'm guessing that in Jesus' eyes the two exclamations are pretty much the same.

But I'm justified, right? The guy's endangering everyone on the road—including me. He's breaking the law. I have a right to call him any name that comes to mind. He deserves it!

Oh, but Christ sees it so differently:

> You have heard that it was said to our ancestors, Do not murder, and whoever murders will be subject to judgment. But I tell you, everyone who is angry with his brother will be subject to judgment. And whoever says to his brother, "Fool!" will be subject to the Sanhedrin. But whoever says, "You moron!" will be subject to hellfire. So if you are offering your gift on the altar, and there you remember that your brother has something against you, leave your gift there in front of the altar. First go and be reconciled with your brother, and then come and offer your gift. (Matt. 5:21–24 HCSB)

Here's the deal. My angry words interrupt relationship. They sever my relationship with another person (even if he's just in the car next to me), and they sever my relationship with God.

But doesn't God get angry? I like how William Wilberforce Rand answers this in *A Dictionary of the Holy Bible*: "Anger is in Scripture frequently attributed to God . . . not that he is liable to those violent emotions which this passion produces, but figuratively speaking . . . he punishes the wicked with severity of a superior provoked to anger."[1]

Rand identifies the crux of the issue: sure Texting Guy is wrong, and I'd love to see him get the fat, juicy, moving violation he deserves. But it's not up to me. There's enough sin and anger in me to invoke God's wrath. It's only by His grace and mercy that I don't get what *I* deserve. Rather than being quick to point out someone else's sin in what I consider justified anger, I ought to be busy seeking God's forgiveness for myself—because I've earned *His* justified anger.

Aw, Stuff It!

Now, let me give a nod to pop psychology here. When David tells us to refrain from anger, when James tells us to be slow to anger, and when Paul tells us to put it away, none of them is telling us to stuff it down deep within our hearts and tamp it down well, giving it a place to fester until it spews out of us like Kilauea. Common sense tells us this can't be right.

One psychologist I interviewed several years ago used this word picture I've never forgotten: stuffed anger is like an egg in a microwave. If its shell isn't pricked to release the increasing steam pressure, the egg is guaranteed to explode its sticky, gooey, stinky contents all over. It's a given.

So what does it mean to *put away* anger? According to Greek scholar Archibald Thomas Robertson, it means to "lay aside like old clothes."[2] I love this word picture because I'm a total clothes horse. Ask anyone. I love pretty, stylish, colorful clothes. I also love keeping them fresh and new for years. The only thing that can entice me to lay aside my favorite old clothes is when I either grow or shrink (my weight does the yo-yo thing way too often) to the point that I can no longer wear them.

That's what it's like with anger. We need to make the choice to let it go—because it doesn't fit us anymore, not if we're going to follow Christ. Anger encumbers us like my pair of raggedy blue jeans from the 1980s. The best thing we can do is follow Christ's example and lay down our right to exact justice for ourselves.

Just like in our clothing analogy, only once we lay aside the old can we put on the new—which, as Paul reminds us, is quite beautiful: "Put on then . . . compassionate hearts, kindness, humility, meekness, and patience" (Col. 3:12).

How do we get to the point where we're willing and able to change our clothes?

Vengeance Is God's

The first solution is to quit focusing on what or who makes us angry. We need to stop fueling our own anger with thoughts of revenge, thoughts of righting wrongs done against us. Like our character Revenge should have done, we need to separate ourselves from people who are fueling our anger for their own purposes.

How?

By claiming God's promise: "I will contend with those who contend with you" (Isa. 49:25).

Similarly, Paul quotes from Deuteronomy 32:35 when he writes, "Friends, do not avenge yourselves; instead, leave room for His wrath. For it is written: 'Vengeance belongs to Me; I will repay,' says the Lord" (Rom. 12:19 HCSB).

Our friend Revenge was right in one thing, she was right to carry her grievances to Christ—not as accusations of Him, but as a request that His righteousness exact justice for her. In the passage from Deuteronomy 32 the Lord reassures His people, "'The day of their calamity is at hand, and their doom comes swiftly.' For the LORD will vindicate his people and have compassion on his servants" (vv. 35–36).

He is, after all, the God of righteousness. Jeremiah 33:15 makes this clear: when Christ the "righteous Branch" enters the scene, He will "execute justice and righteousness."

The thing is that we resent waiting for justice—every bit as much as we hate waiting for mercy and all the other good gifts from God's hand. The day when God does execute decisive judgment against transgressors will be fearful. Prophets trembled as they caught glimpses of the measured fury meted out by the righteous God on that day. In setting aside our anger like a change of clothes, we leave room for the wrath of God to act rightly when that moment comes.

Forgiving

While we're waiting, Christ gives us a task to keep us fully engaged. We'll only be free of self-destructive anger when we relinquish it to Him and replace it with forgiveness.

Paul continues that thought after he tells us what to put on in place of wrath: "[Just] as the Lord has forgiven you, so you also must forgive. And above all these put on love, which binds everything together in perfect harmony. And let the peace of Christ rule in your hearts, to which indeed you were called in one body. And be thankful" (Col. 3:13–15).

We could easily feel seething anger at what sinners have stolen as they've sinned against us—all the peace, joy, and freedom we've missed. That wouldn't be fitting for the Christ-follower. Think of Christ's instruction, "And whenever you stand praying, forgive, if you have anything against anyone, so that your Father also who is in heaven may forgive you your trespasses" (Mark 11:25).

He did this by striking example—although He had no trespasses of His own to be forgiven. Think of the anguish He was experiencing at the cross. Then consider the sacrifice it took to gasp these words: "Father, forgive them, for they know not what they do" (Luke 23:34). So, yes, He knows how difficult what He's asking is for us.

This forgiveness, offered by our choice to someone who may not even ask for it, ultimately frees us. It shuts off the microwave that builds up steam inside the eggshells of our hearts.

Then Christ makes a marvelous exchange of clothing for us: His peace for our distress. It's the peace that finally gives the disquieted heart the satisfaction of rest.

And Now Back to the Studio . . .

My embattled, bruised child, revenge is never sweet. It is bitter. It has nearly destroyed you. It is within My power to free you from it. But first You must trust Me.

Trust You? How?

Do You believe that, as the Son of God, I have the ultimate authority in the universe and that one day I will judge every soul with absolute justice?

I believe.

Now, do you acknowledge that, as a member of the human race, you are just as guilty of breaking My Father's laws as anyone who has transgressed against you? Do you realize that just as those who abused you in your early life, just as your sister, the Producer, and Ange have misused you horribly today, so even you have no right to stand before Me?

I'm guilty. There's no denying that. My gun lies here at my feet.

Then, I offer you forgiveness, a right relationship with Me, and the promise that while My mercy will stay with you, My justice will, one day, exact payment for every wrong done against you.

One day? Not today? Not right now?

No. Can you live with that?

I can and I will.

Then you are free.

Free? I'm FREE!

Yes, free, but not without a task to pursue. It will not be easy.

Anything! Anything at all.

It is within your power, now, to forgive those whom you have every right to condemn. As you do, you will find that, in place of anger, My peace will sprout up. Will you do it? Will you choose to forgive?

Discussion Questions

1. Remember that anger is like a puppet master, pulling the strings and getting us to act in ways that are self-destructive. How does James 1:20–21 equip us to cut the strings? In what areas of your life do you need to act on that counsel?

2. What comfort can you take in reading the promise from Isaiah 49:25? What does it mean to you that God will not allow wrongs done against you to go unpunished forever?

3. What role does forgiveness play in breaking the power of anger over us? Whom do you need to forgive? How will you go about offering forgiveness? Does it matter whether the person asks for or accepts your offer? Why or why not?

Chapter 15

How Can I Represent You to a Skeptical World?

By the time Revenge settles down from sobbing gratefully in the Guest's arms, the crew is ready to link the next interview. Everyone is anxious to return to normalcy on set. That is, everyone except the Producer, who skulked out of the building as soon as she could, abdicating her role. The Reporter speaks quickly and decisively.

> Floor Director, Gretta. You've got to produce the rest of this project.

> I couldn't do it. I'd be afraid it'd be too much, and I'd fall off the wagon. I'd become someone I hate again. It's not worth the risk.

> You've got to. We can't stop now. Besides, your gifts are wasted as the Floor Director. You're capable of more. You have our support, right crew? Three cheers for Gretta—back in management, where she belongs.

Gretta directs a shrug toward the Guest. She sees Him wink—ever so slightly. Cam pats Gretta's shoulder as she leaves her position beside him and tentatively takes charge of the control room.

Well, then, team, let's do this. Reporter, who's up next?

We have Silenced in Shadowville, which obviously is not her real location. She asks that her face not appear and that her voice be disguised.

Noted. We can do it postproduction. For now, let's see and hear her. Everyone ready? We go live in five, four, three . . .

Hello, Silenced? Welcome. You're live with our Special Guest.

Thank You for taking my question, Sir. I have been desperate to receive direction.

Hello, My Child. I am glad to see you. Tell Me, what has you feeling silenced? That verb could not be a greater misnomer for you. I created you to have a powerful voice.

That's the thing. How can I use that voice? How can I be the person You created me to be, when You go and plant me in a place where everyone thinks I'm an ignoramus for believing You? When I try to speak, I'm silenced. What good can I be here? Won't You move me somewhere else—somewhere more receptive to receiving the truth?

You wasted no time in getting to your question. But please, start at the beginning, so the viewers can understand.

The beginning? Okay. I've always defined myself as an intellectual, a scientist, a truth seeker. In the complex patterns of the molecules I studied as an undergraduate, I couldn't help but recognize that there has to be an Intelligence behind such perfect order. I read widely on the topic, and through my studies I met You. Today, I hold a doctorate in molecular biology. I'm an associate professor.

Yes, I gifted you with an especially inquisitive and bright mind. I am so pleased when you make the most of the intellectual resources I have given to you.

Sometimes, those resources don't seem like much of a gift, if You will forgive my saying so.

How so?

You gave me the aptitude and passion for a profession where my peers, even my students, discredit me for believing in such an archaic concept as a Creator, let alone a God Who makes a claim on my life. Because of my beliefs, I am censured constantly. I am considered a fool. I have been denied a full professorship even though I more than earned it with my publications and my professional research.

I see.

So, how can I be a light for You in a place where darkness refuses to give way to any glimmer of light at all?

The Reporter nods and jumps into the conversation.

Sir, that's a question we don't need to be a molecular biologist to ask. I've experienced it in the news business. I've worked in some newsrooms where I'm not allowed to post a Scripture verse on my bulletin board. Probably everyone who works or teaches or has interactions in the community outside the church has had the same experience. Aren't You appalled at how our culture has written You off—and us with You?

Actually, I would have to say I told you so. Before I left for the cross, I told My followers the world would be vehemently opposed to them. After all, the world hates Me, why would they not hate you if you follow Me? Why are you shocked?

But isn't there anything we *can* do?

O ne of those ludicrous predictions of the day and hour Christ would return had just come and gone. I was watching a network TV news broadcast—feeling embarrassed that such a bogus notion had been publicized in the name of Christianity. To introduce the story that the world hadn't ended after all, the reporter looked into the camera and said, "Misguided believers were looking for a rescue—an escape. Even yet, they're expecting to be swept away to some glorious future while the rest of us are left to mop up cataclysmic destruction down here."

I wanted to scream at the TV: *You don't get it! You just don't get it!* Her characterization of believers astounded me. I am one. And I can assure you, she couldn't have had it more turned around.

We take no joy in the fact that people who choose not to trust Christ will be left to the coming disaster. The crux of the matter is this: where this world is leading, we Christians are not going to follow. We can't, because we know better. The path the world is on does lead to destruction (although I'd challenge anyone who thinks he knows exactly when that will happen to check his facts against Christ's promise that *no one* will know even up until the moment He returns [Mark 13:32]).

The problem is that, by nature, people ensconced in the kingdom of darkness don't react well to being interrupted by light. Yet, because of our glowingly reborn natures in Christ, we can't help but light the way for captives to the only safe path to freedom.

All this sets us up to be at odds with the world's system—and with individuals in the world. Jesus did tell us to expect as much in John 15:19–20: "If you were of the world, the world would love you as its own; but because you are not of the world . . . the world hates you. Remember the word that I said to you: 'A servant is not greater than his master.' If they persecuted me, they will also persecute you."

The problem comes when we become serious about being Christ-followers as opposed to remaining silent witnesses living introverted and incognito among the perishing. When we get serious, we can't keep silent. That sets us up for heaps of trouble.

What They Think of Christ

What that end-of-the-world news item did for me was give me a snapshot of how people in the world see us. I often tell my writing students to try on another perspective for size. In learning what motivates someone else, they'll reach that audience more effectively. It's great counsel here, as we seek our place in a society that's openly hostile to Christ.

So what do those apart from Christ see when they see Him—or us?

First, they see Him as roughly equal to the primitive ignorance of mythology. They consider God as insufficient an explanation for the existence of this world as they'd consider Zeus. Worse for us, they consider His followers about as relevant or as informed as those who sacrificed for safety, crop protection, or fertility in ancient Rome's Pantheon.

If that's their perspective, is it any wonder they consider Christ-followers ignorant?

What else do they see? At least in American/Western culture, we've been conditioned to revere the right to pursue happiness, freedom, and independence. (If you're from another culture, you probably already know this about Americans.)

So often, though, Christ's call on a Christian's life appears to curb absolute freedom by inviting us to depend on Him and to exchange momentary ecstasy for abiding joy. From the outside, unbelievers see us and our Lord as a major buzz kill.

But that's not all. There's one more anger trigger that's bigger than them all. In our generation that worships tolerance of every preference or viewpoint, the only ones subject to intolerance are those who hold unyielding beliefs.

Oh wait. That could describe us. The biggest issue this generation has with Christ is that He refuses to be *one among many* ways to God. He is "the" Way. Unique. Beyond equal. He said so. We Christians are the messengers of that message, but we aren't the initiators. We didn't make it up. God's justice required it. Yet when we take our stand on it as "the" truth, we're written off as intolerant, elitist, bigoted, fanatical.

So that's how coworkers, politicians, media, and our greatest adversaries see Christians. Ignorant, intolerant, weak and in need of a crutch, killjoys, unconcerned, deluded, outdated, irrelevant, escapists. In all this, they are deluded by the enemy.

Ashamed?

With the world in such a powerfully hideous grip, though, what can we do to change their eternal destinies? Here's how God answered His prophet Ezekiel who had that exact concern. It's a challenge with implications to us:

> And whether they hear or refuse to hear (for they are a rebellious house) they will know that a prophet has been among them. And you, son of man, be not afraid of them, nor be afraid of their words, though briers and thorns are with you and you sit on scorpions. Be not afraid of their words, nor be dismayed at their looks, for they are a rebellious house. And you shall speak my words to them, whether they hear or refuse to hear, for they are a rebellious house. (Ezek. 2:5–7)

Boy, does the description "a rebellious house" give an accurate description of postmodern thought. They're adamant. They're armed with briers and thorns (nuisances) and with scorpions (life-threatening poisons). With all that, we're supposed to be unafraid? Really?

Apparently, though, the power in speaking the truth is supernatural in origin—not from this world at all. It can't be legislated away, extinguished by darkness, stung away, or poisoned into oblivion. So, even in the face of opposition, we *can* speak God's unchanging truth.

But the other part of that Scripture reminds us that when we speak in obedience to God's direction, we aren't responsible for our hearers' reactions. Those honestly seeking truth will recognize it, while scoffers continue to scoff and rebels continue to rebel. It's rather like the different responses to Christ's offer of forgiveness in the previous chapter.

The key to what we can do is found in listening to the words God would have us speak to them (note, only *His* words carry life-giving power) and in being unashamed to speak them.

That part, our being unashamed, is our big challenge. I wrote this in *Praying Like Jesus,* as I reflected on how I feel on an airplane when asked what I do for a living. What I do is write Christian books, teach Bible classes, and speak at Christian conferences. Saying that too early shuts the door tightly before I can get a toe in. So, here's what I do:

> I try to listen to the person in the seat beside me, to prayer-fully consider how best to broach the topic of faith, to listen for God's direction in how best to "give the reason for the hope that [I] have" (1 Peter 3:15). [1]

That might sound simplistic, but it's true. If we barge into someone's private space without earning a hearing, we're assured a negative response. The fact is that, spiritually speaking, until a heart is quickened by God's Spirit, it simply cannot tune in to the truth. A dead heart absolutely will remain dead. Only the life of God's Spirit can breathe into a spiritually dead corpse and equip its ears to hear. So, I don't think I have it all wrong if I try to listen first, pray for God's direction, then step through the opening He places before me to speak unashamedly about Him.

I bet you're thinking, *That's good for you, Julie. You're a professional Christian. But I'm like Silenced, like the Reporter—I'm censured in my workplace for the most innocuous comment.*

I do believe the principle is sound for you, too. Look at the apostle Paul who—despite being stoned, beaten, imprisoned, and worse—could say, "I am not ashamed of the gospel, for it is the power of God for salvation" (Rom. 1:16).

I love what preacher Dr. R. Newton says to challenge us to put away our natural tendencies to be ashamed of our faith and our inclinations to shy away from being considered ignorant because of Christ.

> Where is the philosopher who is ashamed to own the God
> of Nature? Where is the Jew that is ashamed of Moses? or
> the Moslem that is ashamed of Mahomet? and shall the
> Christian . . . be ashamed of Christ? God forbid! No! let me
> be ashamed of myself, let me be ashamed of the world, and
> let me blush at sin; but never, never, let me be ashamed of
> the gospel of Christ![2]

Newton makes a great point. The atheist, agnostic, or worshipper of
nature isn't ashamed to promote his agenda. Neither is the Muslim
ashamed to pray toward Mecca. So, why should we, who have the Truth
living within us and energizing us, be ashamed to speak His name boldly
in the public arena?

Intellect Engaged

Possibly because of my many associations within the Christian world,
I know dozens of intellectually prepared, thinking Christians—people
who are well educated and well versed in the wisdom of God's Word. My
great goal is to be among them. So, I dig into the Bible and read widely
to be able to both understand it for myself and be equipped to explain
it intelligently.

The key is to be prepared, to know what's in God's Word (and what
isn't). I love that Peter challenges us:

> In your hearts honor Christ the Lord as holy, always being
> prepared to make a defense to anyone who asks you for
> a reason for the hope that is in you; yet do it with gentle-
> ness and respect, having a good conscience, so that, when
> you are slandered, those who revile your good behavior in
> Christ may be put to shame. (1 Pet. 3:15–16)

Sounds a little like the Boy Scout motto, doesn't it? Always be prepared when someone asks for a reasoned, thoughtful account of your faith in Christ.

It also reminds me of the training I went through as a spokesperson for a major corporation. I learned to prepare my message in advance so that if someone asked about the company I wouldn't stammer around and come off as unbelievable. I learned to be polished enough in my presentation to be clear in presenting the message briefly, concisely, completely.

As I prepared for my corporate job, so we as Christians can prepare our responses to likely questions about Christ and our faith. If this is an area where you feel deficient but want to buttress your knowledge, brush up using one of the many handbooks of Christian apologetics. Several solid publishers (including InterVarsity Press, Broadman & Holman, and Baker Publishing) have compiled great books for lay readers on the subject. You don't need to be a theologian to read and understand them.

The second aspect of Peter's instruction also is crucial. When we speak, we do it with gentleness and respect, so people can't find fault in our behavior toward them. Bible college president Joe Stowell gives a clear word picture to help us understand this. First he notes that today's Christians have a reputation for anger at political policies that "condone and even embrace sin." But anger seldom characterized Christ's reputation. In His Bible study e-book, *Joe Stowell on Christian Living,* Stowell illustrates:

> America has a nickname for tow trucks: wreckers. In England, the tow trucks all have one big word printed on them: RECOVERY. Same vehicle, same instruments, same mission—totally different perspective. We say, There goes a wrecker. They say, Here comes recovery. A lot of people in the body of Christ move like a wrecker, but Christ came on a recovery mission.[3]

To continue Stowell's analogy, if our goal is to be as offensive as possible and keep as many people out of God's kingdom as we can, we'll go through life as wreckers. But, if our goal is to be like Christ, we'll seek to recover souls from the road to destruction by balancing His truth with His grace.

This is a tall order, and a costly one. Paul asks, "Who is sufficient for these things?" (2 Cor. 2:16). The cost of standing for Christ without compromise may seem extreme in this world. But I'm more concerned about consequences that'll last a lot longer.

Jesus made the choice clear: "Everyone who acknowledges me before men, I also will acknowledge before my Father who is in heaven, but whoever denies me before men, I also will deny before my Father who is in heaven" (Matt. 10:28–33).

Ouch! I don't want Christ to be ashamed to claim me. Given the choice, I'd rather have my peers here be ashamed of me. So, I'm going to commit to making greater effort in vocally promoting the truth—not to be an offense for the sake of offending, but to be unashamed for the sake of the Gospel.

Now Back to Our Interview . . .

Both women eagerly await the Guest's answer. Before speaking, He meets every eye in the room and on screen—each time peering deeply into His follower's heart.

Would you truly choose to become My representatives to stubborn souls on a path to certain destruction? Would you choose to associate publicly with Me, even when the cost to you is great? Would you choose to take My reputation for yourselves—even among people who hold Me in the lowest esteem? I will not promise to make life easy for you in the short view. But in the long view, I will claim before My Father in heaven all those who claim Me on earth.

Master, we do want to be Your witnesses. We choose to claim You. Show us how.

It is good. I will give you the way: dig into My Word using all your intellect—all your mind and strength. Love the people perishing in the world with My love. Pray about this daily, even moment by moment. Then, and only then, unashamedly tell My story to those who will listen. Do not be timid to claim Me before your peers. In all this, I will be with you, and ultimately no one who trusts Me will be put to shame.

Discussion Questions

1. When and where have you encountered opposition from the world for the sake of Christ? How do the words Jesus spoke in John 15:19–20 challenge you to keep reflecting His light?

2. Describe a time when your conduct was a hindrance to presenting Christ's message to someone. Read 1 Peter 4:12–16. How does Peter's caution apply to you?

3. Read Ezekiel 2. Listen as if God were speaking this message to you. Write your thoughts about how you'll respond to the calling God gives to those who follow Him.

Chapter 16

What Will You Do for Those Who Follow You?

The Reporter massages her temples; fatigue from the long production day is setting in. She is surprised to notice her Guest appears as fresh and energized as He had first thing in the morning, despite all the rigors of their emotional roller-coaster of a day together. She's put off asking the next question as long as she dares.

Sir, I know we've imposed so much on You today. Now, we have a linkup ready that I'm thinking You might not want to take. It's with a high-powered businesswoman who's offering to write us a check to cover the cost of this entire production—her only stipulation is that she must get to talk with You first. She wasn't on the approved list we received from Your advance team, so I'm ashamed to ask. I'm pretty sure our former Producer, or maybe Ange, promised it. It has their fingerprints all over it. Honestly, I didn't know about it until dinner time. But would You maybe be willing to take a few minutes with Shirley-Goodness from Sheboygan? It's okay if You don't want to, but I had to ask.

I have spoken to several individuals today who were not on that list. I see no reason not to hear what Shirley-Goodness has to say. I make it my policy not to turn away anyone who requests an audience. Go ahead and connect us—and be sure the recording is rolling. What I have to tell Shirley-Goodness will have meaning for your viewers as well.

Oh, thank You, Sir. You don't know what this means to us.

You might want to hear how I respond before you thank Me.

Now I'm doubly intrigued! Gretta, did you note all that? Make the link to Sheboygan. We're ready when you are. Remember, Sir, don't say I didn't warn you.

I can handle Myself just fine with someone like Shirley-Goodness.

If You say so. She sure scares me! Looks like we're getting the countdown from the control room. . . . Hello ma'am. It is good to meet you. We have you live here with our Special Guest, just as you requested. Go ahead and address Him directly.

Hello, Guest. Do You know who I am?

Hello, Miss Goodness.

It really is You. How very nice. I'm glad to make Your acquaintance. I've heard so many wonderful things about You over the years that I just had to know if they're true. One hears many things, You know. It never hurts to check them out.

I agree, especially when the company you keep has a track record of overblown statements and half-truths. And the company *you* keep does tend to be unreliable.

You *know* the company I keep?

Yes. I do. I see you each Sunday in your embellished sanctuary. I watch as you sit through lectures on morals, relationships, loving everyone, or practicing the Golden Rule. I see you swivel to one side and the other to spy on others as they watch the speaker. I hear you wonder whether your friend's suit is from the discount store and measure your associate's success by the cut of her hair or the make of her car. I hear the catty chatter among your colleagues when the lecture is over. The half-truths passed. The words better left unsaid. Yes, I certainly do know the company you keep.

That's interesting. I'm glad You called that to my attention. I'll have to be more careful in the future. I hadn't realized You were watching.

Well?

Well, what?

What is it that you wanted to say to Me, now that you see I am Who I claim to be.

That was pretty direct, wasn't it? I wasn't going to dive right in. That's rather bullish. I wanted us to chat a bit first.

Chat about what?

There's a lot about me I wanted You to discover.

Oh?

It wouldn't exactly be suitable for me to tell You all about the wonderful things I could offer You. I mean, I wanted You to ask me about my work, my credentials, and my bank accounts. I wanted You to be at least a little curious about why I might have been willing to underwrite this project. It's not in my nature for me to toot my own horn.

Really? That statement seems incongruous with the name you selected for yourself. You seem to be flaunting your goodness before Me and before the others in this broadcast. Why do you not simply tell Me what you want Me to know?

I could do that—although it wouldn't be nearly as much fun.

I can live with that.

Okay, fine. You already know I'm a churchgoing woman; I haven't missed a Sunday since 1993—except when I'm away on business or that time when I was in the hospital. I've been an entrepreneur since before it was the *en vogue* thing to be.

And I'm good at it. Really, really good. I've made millions. That's opened lots of doors for me. I serve on committees in the community and on corporate boards of directors. I've even been tapped to run for office. When I talk, people listen.

Yes, I know. And?

Here's the thing. I have a lot to offer. Lots of influence. Lots of money. Lots of power. I'm a great person to have on Your team. But like everyone else, I have my price. I do for You, but then You need to do for me. So, I need to know what You have to offer me in return for my service. If I sign on with You and give you access to my valuable resources, what'll You do for me?

The Reporter, Cam, and the control-room crew gasp. They see where this conversation is heading, and their funding with it. They aren't the least surprised with the opening line of their Guest's response.

At last, the question that unveils the motives of your heart. Are you certain you want My true and complete answer? I am afraid you will not enjoy hearing what I have to say.

***

I have to agree with the Reporter here: Shirley-Goodness scares me. She believes her own publicity and thinks of herself ever-so-much-more-highly than she ought. In fact, I created Shirley-G to be as easy to dislike as she is hard to ignore. Her question smacks of pride and ego and self-aggrandizement. *I'm a great catch,* she tells the Lord. *So, what bait are you going to use to reel me in? If You want me to bite, it had better be sashimi grade.*

Her audacity isn't what scares me the most, though. What does? The fact that her question hits too close to my motives. Maybe it's a bit too close to yours, too? Is there one of us who, in her heart, doesn't think that enrolling us in His fighting force would be a great coup for Christ? If we're going to throw ourselves into the fray on His behalf, then shouldn't we be plied with costly gifts? Mercenary soldiers have their price, after all. Too often, so do we.

Listen to how Paul responds:

> For consider your calling, brothers: not many of you were wise according to worldly standards, not many were powerful, not many were of noble birth. But God chose what is foolish in the world to shame the wise; God chose what is weak in the world to shame the strong; God chose what is low and despised in the world, even things that are not, to bring to nothing things that are, so that no human being might boast in the presence of God. (1 Cor. 1:26–29)

Way to win friends and influence people, Paul. Did he just call us *foolish, weak, low, despised nothings* who have absolutely no reason to boast before God?

It's a long way up to God from the bargain basement, the bottom rung, or whatever image you conjure up when you think of being the lowest of the low. But that's the picture we need to have of ourselves if we're to approach God with any question about what He has to offer us. We need to realize we're not negotiating with Him from a position of strength. No! We're throwing ourselves at the base of His throne begging for mercy we could never earn, never deserve, never have the tiniest right to request.

What we deserve, while we're flattened at His feet, is for Him to stomp us into dust. What we get, though, is something different. Not because of what we have to offer, but because of Who He is.

What Makes Us Think We're So Valuable to God?

I suspect before we examine what God will do (and has done) for us, we need to be as clear as He is about our motives. Remember, Paul makes this reminder not to the unregenerate but to Christ-followers. I speak only for myself when I say I need this reminder as much as they did. Surely this doesn't apply to you, too?

As we examine ourselves, what questions ought we to be asking?

1) *Why* do we want what we want? As in the case of our haughty friend Shirley-Goodness, too often our motives are all about ourselves—increasing our bank accounts, our power base, and our value to the community.

2) *What* do we intend to do with the gifts we receive from God? Usually, we want to use them to puff ourselves up, to make others think more highly of us, to lord our successes over friends and coworkers, or to wield more power, more influence, and more self.

James puts his finger on the issue: "You desire and do not have, so you murder. You covet and cannot obtain, so you fight and quarrel. You do not have, because you do not ask. You ask and do not receive, because you ask wrongly, to spend it on your passions" (James 4:2–3). Ouch! So painfully, shamefully right on. I do believe that reminder would be on Christ's lips if He were to answer Shirley-G (and us) for real.

How much better would it be to take the approach of another wealthy woman, Lydia, a seller of purple cloths in the ancient city of Thyatira? Lydia hears Paul's teachings about Christ, and the Lord opens her heart. Dr. Luke, writing the book of Acts, reports what happens next: "After she was baptized, and her household as well, she urged us, saying, 'If you have judged me to be faithful to the Lord, come to my house and stay.' And she prevailed upon us" (Acts 16:15).

Did you catch the difference? Like Shirley-G, Lydia has a great deal to offer—including wealth and influence in her community. But unlike Shirley-G, her heart is on the opposite end of the spectrum. Lydia's offering isn't a condition of signing on with God but a result of serving God. She hears; she realizes her sinfulness; she repents; she submits to baptism; she associates with Christ. Then—and only then—she offers what she has to God. Her motivation is a grateful heart—not a greedy one.

The knowledge that God has chosen to lift her up rather than stomp her down—drives her to beg for the privilege of serving Him. She lavishes her gifts on Him, not to earn her keep, but to express her worship.

That's a subject we'll cover in the next two chapters. But it's a great illustration for us here, if we're to recognize the difference between serving self and serving God.

Doesn't He Promise Us the World?

Tune in to any late-night preacher, and you're liable to hear a vastly different answer to the question we're considering here. Westerners are all about the WIIFM (what's in it for me?). What we may encounter in lots of preaching designed to appeal to the masses is the idea that, since God promises to meet all our needs according to His riches (Phil. 4:19), we're guaranteed to enjoy loads of wealth in this world.

How could that be true when Jesus said of Himself: "Foxes have holes, and birds of the air have nests, but the Son of Man has nowhere to lay his head" (Matt. 8:20). Look what happened to John, Peter, Paul, and the other apostles—imprisonment, torture, martyrdom. So did Paul have it all wrong?

I suppose the key to understanding comes when we add back the rest of his sentence. After "riches" comes "in glory in Christ Jesus." *In glory* may be another way of reminding us to "lay up for yourselves treasures in heaven, where neither moth nor rust destroys and where thieves do not break in and steal" (Matt. 6:20). *In Christ Jesus* reminds us it's all about His kingdom established, His purposes advanced, His will done.

Then as He does promise to meet our need—it may be that He has a clearer understanding of our true need than we do.

God Knows Best

So, then, when we approach God like Lydia did, what *can* we expect Him to do for us? Actually, it's already been done—and it's a doozey. I love the word picture author Anne Graham Lotz paints for us:

> It never occurred to Satan, who ever seeks his own preem-
> inence, that the Creator of the universe would lay down
> His own life in atonement for man's sin. But that's exactly
> what happened. [1]

Wow! We've been looking at our selfish motives, and we now realize we have nothing to be grand or pompous about. But then there's God—the antithesis of all we are. He has *everything* to be grand and pompous about. He is the one and only unchallenged and unequalled Deity. He has every right to demand homage, to wield authority, to satisfy His justice in light of our great offense. And what did He go and do? He gave Himself away—for the lowest of the low. He did this while we were still in filthy bondage to sin, while we had less than nothing to recommend us.

What was His motivation? "God shows his love for us in that while we were still sinners, Christ died for us" (Rom. 5:8).

Love.

God, our Creator, saw our greatest need—a restored relationship with Him. So in love, He gave Himself fully, wholeheartedly. He promised He'd do just that through the prophet Jeremiah:

> Yet *I will certainly bring health and healing* to it and will
> indeed heal them. *I will let them experience the abundance of
> peace and truth.* I will restore the fortunes of Judah and of
> Israel and will rebuild them as in former times. *I will purify
> them from all the wrongs they have committed against Me,* and
> I will forgive all the wrongs they have committed against
> Me, rebelling against Me. This city will bear on My behalf
> a name of joy, praise, and glory before all the nations of

the earth, who will hear of all the good I will do for them. They will tremble with awe because of all the good and all the peace I will bring about for them. (Jer. 33:6–9 HCSB, emphasis added)

Note that the worker in all this is *God*. He doesn't send an underling. He doesn't leave it to us to find a way. He Himself, *brings, restores, purifies, and forgives.*

Let's examine just three of these promises:

- *I will certainly bring health and healing.*
  In studying the Hebrew word, *arûkâ*, that God uses in Jeremiah 33:6, commentator Adam Clarke explains the word picture the original hearers would have associated with *health*: "a plaister [*sic*] as large as the sore."[2] So, from the context we can tell He's promising to provide a medicated wound dressing to heal the broken relationship between the Father and us. The sacrifice of Christ would be as large as our sore—sufficient to cover and heal our greatest ailment—the sin disease.

- *I will purify them from all the wrongs they have committed against Me.*
  He makes two promises here: He'll make us clean (purify), and He'll forgive us. Since we committed the wrongs against Him, and since the sacrifice of Christ was sufficient payment for them, He offers to forgive—to count them as paid in full and remove them from the debt record on our account. This is beautiful. So, if our selfish friend Shirley-G or we confess our sins, He'll accept His own blood as our complete payment.

- *I will let them experience the abundance of good and truth.*
  Listen here for what God values on our behalf. In this statement, we find the most complete answer of what we gain

from becoming His servants: peace with Him, knowledge of the Truth, and the privilege of wearing His name, a name of "joy, praise and glory." In these, He knows we'll find the fulfillment of our greatest needs.

All this clarifies for us the real WIIFM of becoming a Christ-follower: everything (or nothing) else may come along beside, but the real value is in the gift of unadulterated relationship made possible by His death and resurrection.

Now Back to the Studio . . .

Shocking everyone except the Guest, Shirley-Goodness makes a snap decision about how to respond to His baiting words.

Since I asked the question, I should be open to hearing Your answer. That would only be fair. I must say . . . You are different than I had been led to believe. Tougher, somehow. More relevant, too. I think I respect You more knowing that about You than when I thought You were all warm and fuzzy and soft.

That is good. Then, here is My answer. What is in it for you? Certainly not all the things you think you need. But rather everything I know you need: healing and health for your soul, cleansing and purification to cover your sin, and the privilege of experiencing an abundance of good and truth that flows from a personal relationship with Me.

Before I met You, I would have asked how much all that would cost me. I would have thought it sounded too good to be true. But seeing what it cost You, I think something must have changed inside me.

It has.

Then let me ask You this, if You consider me someone who has received these gifts from You, may I please use the resources You've given me to further the cause of Your choosing?

Before I answer, will you do something for Me? Will you stay right there and listen to the next interview? You are not the only one with that question.

Discussion Questions

1. What's the difference between associating with Christ as a mercenary soldier (on the basis of expected rewards) and as a grateful, forgiven child of His? Which have you been? Explain which you choose to be as you go forward.

2. Read 1 Corinthians 1:26–30 where Paul gives us a painful glimpse into exactly how much we had to offer before Christ rescued us. How do you react to this reminder? Why is it important to have an accurate view of yourself as you approach God?

3. What gifts has God given you that you are now able to offer back to Him as acts of service, of gratitude, of love? What specific steps will you take to do that?

Chapter 17

What Purpose Do You Have for Me?

In the control room, brows furrow. Papers riffle. Fingers point. Voices raise. In desperation, Gretta punches the intercom, and her voice booms into the studio where the Reporter and the Guest are chatting softly.

Reporter! Heads up! Check your notes. We're in a crisis here. We have one last linkup before you shoot your wrap, but we can't make the connection.

What do you mean, can't make the connection? It's supposed to be Curious in Columbia, isn't it?

Yeah, we know that. The computer shows a crew was dispatched, but we don't know which crew or where they're supposed to be. We can't raise them through network central dispatch. It's a disaster. Give me your backup info for Curious. Her real name? Her exact location?

Funny thing about that. I don't know where this name came from. I didn't add it to the list. I don't know anything about her.

Excuse Me, if you please. I believe I can shed light on this situation. Curious added her own name to the list. She dispatched the phony crew. And she isn't in Columbia but rather here in the studio. If you expose the small booth behind the curtain that's been our backdrop, you will find the woman who wishes to be called Curious in Columbia. She has been satisfying her curiosity for some time now. I have known about her all along. Also, I suggest you roll tape or whatever it is you do to begin recording.

The curtain parts and a figure emerges. Everyone gasps and snaps to attention in one motion. The woman brushes past the Reporter and comes to an abrupt stop in front of the Guest.

You knew I was there? You knew I was Curious?

I *made* you Curious.

Sir, excuse me for butting in, but *You* know the president of broadcasting from the parent company of our network?

Yes, Reporter, I know all about her. Tell Me, Madam President, did you get your questions answered today?

Mostly. Lots came into focus for me today.

But you have more to ask?

I do. I waited until the others had their opportunities. That's what protocol would require. But I couldn't miss the chance to listen in. I cleared my schedule and arrived before anyone got into the building. I set up a monitor in this obsolete voice-over booth and wrapped the curtain around me. But then You know all that.

Why would you go to all that trouble? I would have been most pleased to talk with you earlier. The crew would have made you comfortable.

Everyone would have been different. You might have shown me only what You wanted me to see. I was interested not only in what would make the final cut, or even what would be on the raw recording, but I had to see and hear how You'd be when the cameras weren't rolling, when the lights were dim and the mood was relaxed.

How did I measure up to your standard?

Oh my, Your responses, Your compassion, Your tenderness, and even Your firmness amaze me. One thing I can't figure, though.

What is that?

Why didn't You crush the Producer and Ange when they attacked You? Surely these formidable guardians of Yours could have pulverized them. Then again, one word from You would have done the same. Why would You let them go? Were you leaving it to me to punish them? How would You have me deal with their impudence?

Curious, You have listened, but you have yet to hear—to understand. Those two have chosen to remain in their prisons of anguish—and it breaks My heart. I have no need for you to exact punishment on them. You rightly say that I am capable of finishing that job. For now, let us leave room for the message of forgiveness and restoration to reach them. There will be a day of punishment if they choose not to repent. But today the offer of grace remains for them—and for you.

I'm not right with You yet, am I?

No. But you may choose to be. Do you wish it to be so?

Oh, yes, My Lord. Until now, I've felt more at ease in darkness than light because darkness didn't expose my sin. But You, in the bright light of Your love and kindness, You show me how much I've missed the standard of perfection. I have a desperate need for You to save me from my many, many transgressions of Your law. Will You? Would You? Please save me today.

I am willing. I welcome you in to My Father's kingdom of light.

Is it true? I can know You and face You unashamed?

That is My gift to those who accept My offer of forgiveness, those who come to Me humbly admitting their sin and seeking atonement from My death on their behalf.

This is so far beyond what I expected. I don't know how to let You know how much this means to me. I want to do something for You. Give You something. Everything. But what can I give You—when You have everything already? I'll do whatever You ask. Only, please tell me, what purpose do You have for me?

As you will recall, Shirley-Goodness asked somewhat the same question. She is still waiting for her answer. I will respond to you both now.

A t least in the Western world, we are a rather comfortable gener-ation—living with not only our basic needs pleasantly satisfied but a slew of our whims and wants fulfilled. I recall some dim notion I picked up years ago in Psych 101 (from studying Maslow's Hierarchy of Needs pyramid) that, once we have our foundational needs of food and shelter, safety and community covered, we tend to turn our attention to higher issues. Among those is the issue of finding our purpose, our reason for being.

If you look around at individuals, churches, corporations, minis-tries, families, even clubs today, you'll find that all of these have become utterly driven by purpose: locating it, maximizing it, fulfilling it, reach-ing for it. To be this preoccupied with purpose, we must indeed feel our more basic needs are happily covered.

While I'm not sure pursuing purpose for purpose's sake is the best use of our energies, I do believe one of the highest pursuits we can set out to fulfill is to know God's reasons for placing us here. Not just to know and be satisfied in the knowing. But rather to know and then to spend our life resources on living up to the plans He has for us.

It's a valid response to the gifts Christ lavishes on us. It's rather like the woman who had been forgiven much who, in an expression of overflowing gratitude, poured out her most expensive perfume on Jesus' feet and wiped them with her hair (John 12:3). We must find some expression for our gratefulness—and how better to do it than a way He would find most pleasing?

You wouldn't be surprised, here, if I reintroduced Jeremiah 29:11: "I know the plans I have for you. . . ." But it's one thing for Him to know His own plans for us. It's quite another for Him to reveal them to us. That, I believe, is at the heart of the questions posed by Curious and Shirley-Goodness—and us, of course. *Now that You've met my most basic need for cleansing and restored relationship with You, please let me in on Your plans for me, God. Let me know, so I can work toward them as my goal.*

One of the clearest answers comes from a familiar prophecy. Even before our journey together you would have recognized these words. You might think they originate in the text of Handel's *Messiah*. Maybe you've even sung these themes. Truthfully, though, Handel didn't craft these lyrics—God did, as part of His message to us through Isaiah:

> The voice of him that crieth in the wilderness, Prepare ye the way of the LORD, make straight in the desert a highway for our God. Every valley shall be exalted, and every mountain and hill shall be made low: and the crooked shall be made straight, and the rough places plain: And the glory of the LORD shall be revealed, and all flesh shall see *it* together: for the mouth of the LORD hath spoken *it*. . . . O Zion, that bringest good tidings, get thee up into the high mountain; O Jerusalem, that bringest good tidings, lift up thy voice with strength; lift *it* up, be not afraid; say unto the cities of Judah, Behold your God! (Isa. 40:3–5, 9 KJV, emphasis added)

I told you it would sound familiar. In this chapter of Isaiah's prophecy, I count five familiar themes from Handel's masterwork.

Now that we've read the passage in the familiar King James cadence, let's break it down in modern language. Let's examine what this lilting passage reveals about the tasks God has for us.

Here to Be Emissaries

"Listen! It's the voice of someone shouting" (Isa. 40:3 NLT).

As I mentioned earlier, in my first job out of graduate school, I was a spokesperson for a Fortune 500 company. I spoke the message the company wanted disseminated to cynical radio DJs, chiseled TV anchors, and grizzled newspaper reporters.

When I called any department, even an executive VP, staff put me right through. Those with rank higher than my entry-level position scrambled to locate info I needed. The doors to the executive suite opened to me—I met with the chairman of the board and all the executive team. It was quite a heady job for a newbie.

A couple of years in, I was promoted to the customer service training department. My job was more responsible, more demanding. But now, when I called those executives, I was rebuffed by junior staffers. Turns out, my access had never been about my merit, but about authority I'd been loaned as spokesperson.

Similarly, for those of us interested in knowing our place in God's plan, Isaiah's vision offers a reminder: The message isn't ours, it's His. The kingdom isn't ours, it's His. The ultimate purpose isn't ours, it's . . . yes again, it's His.

Who are we? Here's the job description I see: we're "someone shouting." In Isaiah 40:9, these shouters carry the label *herald*. That's an odd, archaic word. Today, we might consider a herald as a *spokesperson, envoy, representative, emissary, diplomat, delegate, messenger, courier,* or even an *ambassador.*

Think of it. The ambassador from your country reports in to the United Nations and his (or her) credentials are accepted not on his own merit but on the recommendation and representation of the ruling body of your nation. If the same person were to report to the UN without his government's blessing, he wouldn't be allowed past the public viewing gallery—any more than I as a customer service training manager could claim access to the executive suite. None of the merit that gets him his seat on the council is his, it's only valid when he can back it up with the authority of his president or congress, prime minister or parliament.

Likewise, the herald Isaiah describes comes under the authority of One greater. The herald carries a critical message from that Mighty One. And, in her role as carrier of the message, she is critically important because of Whom she represents. As modern-day heralds representing the kingdom of heaven on earth, we are couriers to this generation, carrying His epic message with eternity-altering implications.

Here to Clear the Way

"Clear the way through the wilderness for the Lord*! Make a straight highway through the wasteland for our God!"* (Isa. 40:3 NLT).

One task of His ambassadors is to be on His advance team, making preparations for Him to enter the scene with pomp and circumstance. "Clear the way," Isaiah says. Pave the highway. Fill in the potholes with asphalt. Make the wasteland blossom. *The Preacher's Outline & Sermon Bible* explains this role in terms that would have been obvious to the original readers of this prophecy.

> This is a picture of the Near East custom of sending ambassadors ahead of a king to announce His coming. A king's visit to an area was a cause for great celebration. Enormous preparations would be made. Either a special road would be built or an existing roadway upgraded and readied for the monarch's appearance. Preparations always included leveling the roadway by filling in the valleys, lowering the hills, and straightening out the crooked sections. All obstacles that lay in the roadway would be removed.[1]

John the Baptist did this in preparing the people of his day for the public ministry of Jesus, the Messiah. Likewise, clearing the way continues to be a key purpose for God's ambassadors to our generation.

We should work to get their hearts ready. Let them know the King is coming. Let them know how He wants to meet with them. Prepare the path for the Lord to make His entrance into their hearts by faith. Show them what He looks like by reflecting His love for them in how we live our lives.

As His reps, we carry His message—speak the words we hear from Him, act in ways that honor Him, think the thoughts He places in our minds. It's the fulfillment of what we considered in Chapter Fifteen about representing Christ to a skeptical world. It gives us the "what" to go along with the "how" we learned earlier.

But are we up to this humongous task?

Here to Carry the News

"O Zion, messenger of good news, shout from the mountaintops! Shout it louder, O Jerusalem. Shout, and do not be afraid" (Isa. 40:9 NLT).

In Isaiah's day, the herald's role was a pleasant one. He wasn't the town crier who carried the everyday, bland gossip or even the foreboding news of an invading army. Not at all. According to James Strong, *bāśar*, the Greek word for "herald" means "to *be fresh*, i.e. *full* (*rosy*, figurative *cheerful*); to *announce* (glad news) :- messenger, preach, publish, shew [*sic*] forth, (bear, bring, carry, preach, good, tell good) tidings."[2]

What is the fresh, cheerful, rosy news we carry from the kingdom of heaven to the people of earth? I love the way the NLT renders its vibrant answer in verses 5, 8–11:

- Your God is coming!
- The glory of the LORD will be revealed.
- All people will see it.
- He brings His reward with Him as He comes.

- He will rule with a powerful arm.
- He will feed His flock like a shepherd.
- He will carry the lambs in His arms, holding them close to His heart.

Who but Christians steeped in God's Word can be ambassadors of the astounding news that the Mighty God is tough and tender, just and merciful, truth and grace?

Isaiah tells us to publish God's message widely, loudly, and without fear. This is great news that we carry—life-giving, fresh, glad, and worthy of publishing using every modern-day tool. I suppose that's one of the many reasons I chose to set our fictional scene in a newsroom. I can't imagine a greater use of our varied modern media than to broadcast the news flash of God's salvation to every inch of the globe.

Many conservative Christians love to media-bash. But what if more of the decision-makers and gatekeepers of major media outlets were to see, hear, and take to heart the good news that we're carrying? What if they heard it first from us? Imagine the potential to reach the world for Christ then.

Similarly, what if we were to make exceptional use of Internet resources to get the word out—to shout it louder, as verse 9 challenges us to do? We're living in an era where everyday people can have a remarkable impact like never before. In this day, heralds of God's kingdom, equipped with the news from His throne, can blast it out from every speaker, monitor, and page on the planet.

Here to Be Sent

"Your God is coming!" (Isa. 40:9 NLT).

So we return to our original question: What is our purpose as those who have trusted Christ and want to express our gratitude back to Him? We are His ambassadors, His advance team. Our message, should we choose to take it up, is clear and concise: God is coming again. He'll establish His kingdom on this planet. On that day, He'll reward those who choose to acknowledge and honor Him today. And, while He's mighty and glorious, powerful and authoritative, He's also gentle and tender—holding His lambs close to His heart.

If this isn't a glad announcement, I don't know what is.

We have the opening and the resources. We have the opportunity. We have the message. We have the heaven-issued credentials to open the doors to us. So, then, are we going to sit around asking our questions, or are we going to sign up to fulfill what we already know as our God-ordained task?

Listen to how Isaiah answers: "I heard the voice of the Lord saying, 'Whom shall I send, and who will go for us?' Then I said, 'Here am I! Send me'" (Isa. 6:8).

And Now Back to the Studio . . .

Shirley-Goodness, are you on the line?

I am here.

Curious, are you ready?

My ears are open, my Lord.

Reporter, how about you? Gretta? Cam? Gen? Mikey? This is for you, too.

As if they have but one voice among them, everyone answers:

We're listening.

Good. Each of you understands the message of the Gospel— the good news of salvation to be announced to every soul.

We understand.

Now, you have a responsibility to do something with that knowledge. My Father has equipped you with gifts and talents, abilities and opportunities. Shirley-Goodness, you have been entrusted with wealth that can advance My cause. Curious, you and so many on your staff have been entrusted with a mighty means of transmitting My message. Reporter, you have a reputation people trust. Gretta, you carry the message of how I am able and willing to remove regret and restore broken lives. Cam, you have the heart of one who knows only I can satisfy your deepest longings. Mikey, you have the power to amplify My message of unconditional love. Gen, you have the creativity to give people a fresh view of Who I Am and Who I can become in their lives. Likewise, your viewers and many of those women who asked their questions have unique, specially chosen gifts. The Spirit Who took up residence in you when you were transferred from darkness to light, has planted in you these seeds that will bear sweet and juicy fruit befitting My kingdom.

Heads nod, but no one is able to speak. After a brief pause, their Master continues with a firmer, yet still tender, tone.

All day I have listened to your questions. Now, I will ask My question of you: "Whom shall I send, and who will go into this alien world as My ambassador?"

Discussion Questions

1. As the drama unfolded, Julie envisioned several times where characters were surprised by a fresh insight about Christ's character. Curious, for example, was surprised at His wisdom and knowledge. Shirley-Goodness was surprised at His strength and power. What fresh insights or reminders have you received about His character from listening to His words?

2. In 1 Corinthians 12:7, Paul reminds us that the Holy Spirit gives each of us spiritual gifts for a specific purpose. First, note that purpose. Then make a chart. In one column, list the gifts and talents Christ has loaned to you; in a second column, list the ways you'll use those gifts for the purpose God intends. Leave a third column free to record results and observations once you've seen Him work through those gifts.

3. The question, "Whom shall I send as a messenger to this people? Who will go for us?," comes from Isaiah 6:8 (NLT). Read the context, beginning with verse 1. Ask God's Spirit to make the scene come alive for you. Journal what you believe He is asking you to do for Him and how you intend to respond.

Chapter 18

What Can I Offer You?

Gretta, now fully adapted to her new role, has energy levels running high among the crew as she helps them ready the last shot of the day. The Reporter rereads her notes and hits send from her tablet to transmit the script for her wrap-up. The Teleprompter Operator acknowledges receipt by punching up the first few lines so they appear on the beam-splitter glass mounted in front of camera one's lens. Gretta activates the intercom.

Cam, Reporter, are you ready to shoot the last word? Guest, You'll still be in the shot, if You don't mind sitting for us just a little longer. This should be pretty straightforward, and then, if You'd be willing, we'd love for You to be our Guest for a wrap party.

I would be most pleased to remain with you for the duration.

Excellent! Okay then, cue teleprompter. Gen, bring up the graphics. Roll stationary cameras. Cam, you're on for the specialty shots. Reporter, since I'm replacing Producer, we don't have a floor director, so you'll need to follow the camera lights yourself. We'll start the first take in four, three, two . . .

My dear viewers, this has been a most remarkable day for us here and in our various remote locations. I can't say I've ever done an interview that has had more impact on *my* life. I don't expect I ever will again. After all, we've just heard from the One Who created us, the One Who is most familiar with our hearts' deepest questions. Our Special Guest made Himself available to us and, despite the efforts of those who tried to interrupt our interview, He's been gracious and truthful in answering each individual personally. As I've been reviewing the way I want to express my gratitude to Him for being here, words penned thousands of years ago by the poet David seem a more fitting wrap-up than I could prepare myself:

> I will give thanks to the LORD with my whole heart;
> I will recount all of your wonderful deeds. . . .
> The LORD is a stronghold for the oppressed,
> a stronghold in times of trouble.
> And those who know your name put their trust in you,
> for you, O LORD, have not forsaken those who seek you.
> Sing praises to the LORD, who sits enthroned in Zion!
> Tell among the peoples his deeds! (Ps. 9:1, 9–11)

I'm sure you can tell from that beautifully crafted poem that it expresses perfectly Who He is and how thankful our whole crew is for His trustworthiness, His compassion and kindness, and His fairness in the way He deals with us. You may recall that we started the day with my question, *What do You want from me?* But that seems so self-serving now, because it was all about me. So, with His permission I'd like to rephrase it to be all about Him—and to express what I believe His answer would be. May I, Sir?

Yes, Reporter, I like where you are going with this. Go ahead; ask and answer your newly worded question.

My Lord, what can I offer You? All I have, You have given to me. The only thing truly my own is my voice, which I choose to use like the psalmist did. I choose to tell the truth about You to everyone who will listen. If the word *amazing* weren't so overused, it might begin to express how I feel as I look at You right here in the studio where I work every day. Now that I see You, I realize how utterly mind-blowing it is for a mere mortal to sit before Your majesty. I'm humbled and so grateful. You are magnificent. I don't say that just because of the solutions You offered to each one You met today. But, after a fraction of a moment in Your presence, I could think of nothing other than bowing to give You the honor You're due. For being Who You are, and for allowing me to tell others about You, I thank You; thank You . . . *thank You.*

Cut. That's a take. One time through was all we needed. Reporter, you're a pro. Good job everyone. Now, let's party!

After unhooking microphones and stepping over cables, the Guest and studio crew join the control room staff at the back of the cavernous room. Curious' personal chef has arranged a gourmet spread—funded by Shirley-Goodness. One Recording Engineer remains at his station to back up the video files. Everyone else clusters close to the Guest, Who comments on the buffet.

You set a lovely table, Curious. Thanks to Shirley-Goodness for providing the resources. It is a fitting offering from you both. If you please, may I offer a blessing over the food?

We'd be honored if you would, Sir.

For these gifts from Your hand, our Father, and for those who graciously prepared them, we are most grateful.

A chorus of amens follows, and the crew is about to dig in when the Guest lifts His hands over them.

Next time, let us meet in My studio. I believe you will find it most lustrously appointed. I will notify you soon, when preparations are complete for your arrival.

With that, He and His flashing host of bodyguards vanish. In the same instant the Recording Engineer pipes in over the intercom:

Guys, didn't we test everything? The audio is great from the studio and all the locations. But I hate to tell you that every time the shot includes our Guest, a light emanating somehow from *within* Him obscures His face. I can't find any way to compensate. What're we going to do?

I'm not surprised.

Gretta grabs the Reporter by the arm.

What're you saying? Why didn't you tell us if you knew something we didn't know?

I'm saying that we've probably just experienced a glimpse into that studio He talked about—the lustrous one in His city. You know, where "night will be no more," where "the Lord God will be their light" (Rev. 22:5). He *is* the ultimate pure light. So, it shouldn't surprise us if His light overwhelms our ability to record it. I say we run with it just as we shot it. I'm thinking it may illuminate our viewers in a way words and pictures alone never could.

You have a point. Guess we don't have an option. So, we go with it?

Yep. I'm good with that.

Well, then everyone . . . that's a wrap!

Discussion Questions

1. One of the ways the Reporter responded to Christ was to offer Him the honor He's due. Read Revelation 4:1–11, where John sees the ascended Christ in all His glory and hears the worship that is repeated around His throne. How does this scene

impact your desire to offer Christ honor? What will you do about it?

2. The closing scene of the drama in this chapter looks a little like what two disciples experienced in Luke 24:28–32. Read that scene. What does it mean for our hearts to "burn within us" as we hear God's Word explained? Tell of a time when that feeling was especially pronounced for you.

3. The invitation to meet God at His place is open to each soul. There's a glimpse of what He's preparing to welcome us home in Revelation 21:1–7. Read the passage and then decide today what you're going to do about His invitation to join Him one day in His heavenly home.

Postscript from the Author, AKA "Reporter"

I want to thank you, reader, for sticking with me in my wild, fanciful imagining of what it would be like to be a modern woman coming face to face with Christ in *The GOD Interviews*. While the specific interactions between "the Guest" and the questioning women were figments of my imagination, I believe you'll find in them the ring of truth. As I expected at the outset, this has been my interview of a lifetime.

What I hope you've discovered along with me is that Jesus Christ—God with Us—does have a passion to interact with us one on one. That's all part of the personal relationship He opened to us through His death and resurrection.

Don't take my word for it. Look at how He interacted with individuals while He walked the earth: Zacchaeus, the woman at the well, Nicodemus, Mary and Martha of Bethany along with their brother Lazarus, Nathaniel, Peter, John, Pilate, even the vengeful Pharisees, and Saul/Paul of Tarsus. His conversations with them were real, gritty, laced with details only their up-close-and-personal Creator could possibly know.

While we're unlike these people in that we probably won't see our God's face this side of eternity, we do hear His voice speaking unmistakably to us from the pages of His Word. And, since the Spirit of the Living God dwells within us by faith, His promptings ring true in the centers of our being.

So, then, our challenge is to listen for His voice—His words of encouragement and uplift, His course corrections and warnings, His answers to our deepest questions. He does speak to us today—because lovingly, uniquely He crafted each of us to fit the tapestry of His plan. The responsibility and choice to listen, though, He leaves to us.

After digging deep into the Word to extrapolate His answers in preparation to write what you've just read, I've made a decision of life-changing proportions. This study refreshed my sense of just how clearly He addresses our personal heart-cries in the pages of the Bible. So, I'm redoubling my efforts to tune in to my Special Guest and His written Word every day of the rest of my life.

I pray that will be your response, too.

Blessings to you, my treasured friend!
Julie-Allyson

Endnotes

Chapter 1

1. Matthew George Easton, *Illustrated Bible Dictionary: And Treasury of Biblical History, Biography, Geography, Doctrine, and Literature* (London: T. Nelson and Sons, 1897), WORD*search* CROSS e-book, under: "Justice of God."

2. Michael J. Wilkins, *NIV Application Commentary, New Testament* (Grand Rapids: Zondervan, 2004), under "Matthew. Matthew 5:38–42."

Chapter 2

1. Adam Clarke, *A Commentary and Critical Notes* (New York: Abingdon-Cokesbury Press, 1826), WORD*search* CROSS e-book, under: "Jeremiah 29."

2. "Doctors Say Man Found Alive 1 Week After Crash Is On The Mend," *CBS Los Angeles*, October 6, 2011, http://losangeles.cbslocal.com/2011/10/06/doctors-say-man-found-alive-1-week-after-crash-is-on-the-mend.

Chapter 3

1. Adam Clarke, *A Commentary and Critical Notes* (New York: Abingdon-Cokesbury Press, 1826), WORD*search* CROSS e-book, under: "Matthew 3."

2. Matthew George Easton, "Repentance," in *Illustrated Bible Dictionary: And Treasury of Biblical History, Biography, Geography, Doctrine, and Literature* (London: T. Nelson and Sons, 1897), WORD*search* CROSS e-book, under: "Repentance."

3. Alfred Edersheim, *Sketches of Jewish Social Life in the Days of Christ* (London: The Religious Tract Society, 1876), WORD*search* CROSS e-book, under: "Chapter 10."

4. Trent C. Butler, ed., *Holman Bible Dictionary* (Nashville, TN: Holman Bible, 1991), WORD*search* CROSS e-book, under: "Repentance."

5. Warren W. Wiersbe, *With the Word Bible Commentary* (Nashville: Thomas Nelson, 1997, c1991), under "Joel 2:1."

Chapter 4

1. Mark Water, ed., *Encyclopedia of Bible Facts* (Chattanooga, TN: AMG, 2004), WORD*search* CROSS e-book, page 641.

2. Thomas Nelson, *The Woman's Study Bible* (Nashville: Thomas Nelson, 1997, c1995) under "Is 43:8."

Chapter 5

1. *A Treasury of Great Preaching* (Austin, TX: WORD*search* Corp., 2005), WORD*search* CROSS e-book, under: "The Justice of God in the Damnation of Sinners."

2. Charles Ryrie, *Basic Theology: A Popular Systematic Guide to Understanding Biblical Truth* (Chicago: Moody Press, 1986), WORD*search* CROSS e-book, 319.

Chapter 7

1. "Deus ex machina," in *The American Heritage Dictionary of the English Language* (Hughton Miffin, 2011), www.answers.com/topic/deus-ex-machina.

Chapter 8

1. Thomas Nelson, *Woman's Study Bible* (Nashville: Thomas Nelson, 1997, c1995), under "Is 41:1."

2. Earl D. Radmacher, Ronald Barclay Allen, and H. Wayne House, *The Nelson Study Bible: New King James Version*. Includes Index (Nashville: T. Nelson Publishers, 1997), under "Isaiah 40:27."

3. Julie-Allyson Ieron, *The Overwhelmed Woman's Guide to . . . Caring for Aging Parents* (Chicago: Moody, 2008), 155.

Chapter 9

1. Anne Graham Lotz, "God's Love," Daily Devotional for March 7, AnGel Ministries, at http://www.annegrahamlotz.com/resources/daily-devotional/3/7/.

Chapter 10

1. Hannah Whitall Smith, *The God of All Comfort*, WORD*search* CROSS e-book, 101.

2. *Your Dictionary: The Dictionary You Can Understand* keyword "comfort," http://www.yourdictionary.com/comfort.

3. William E. Vine, *Vine's Expository Dictionary of Old Testament and New Testament Words* (Nashville, TN: Thomas Nelson, 1940), WORD*search* CROSS e-book, under: "Live (To)."

4. Listed in The Ministry of Lisa Copen, http://chronicillnesssupport.wordpress.com/.

Chapter 12

1. Josh McDowell, *Skeptics Who Demanded a Verdict* (Wheaton, IL: Tyndale, 1989), PDF electronic edition, 7. (If you'd like to read more about Lewis's journey into "following the truth to wherever it leads," McDowell's booklet is available for free

download on his website: http://www.josh.org/site/c.ddKDIMNtEqG/b.4172663/
k.624E/Can_I_Trust_the_Bible.htm.)

2. Trent C. Butler, ed., *Holman Bible Dictionary* (Nashville: Holman Bible
Publishers, 1991), WORDsearch CROSS e-book, under: "Truth."

Chapter 14

1. William Wilberforce Rand, ed., *A Dictionary of the Holy Bible* (New York:
American Tract Society, 1859), WORD*search* CROSS e-book, under: "Anger."

2. Archibald Thomas Robertson, A.M., D.D., LL.D., Litt. D., *Word Pictures in the
New Testament* (Nashville, TN: Broadman Press, 1930), WORD*search* CROSS e-book,
under: "Colossians 3:8."

Chapter 15

1. Julie-Allyson Ieron, *Praying Like Jesus: Discovering the Pattern of Godly Prayer*,
Updated 2nd Edition (Park Ridge, IL: Joy Media, 2010), WORD*search* CROSS e-book,
under: "Chapter 43. Holy, But Not Holier Than Thou."

2. Elon Foster, quoted in *New Cyclopaedia of Prose Illustrations. 1st ser.*,
WORD*search* CROSS e-book, under: "2624. Gospel, Ashamed of the."

3. Joe Stowell, *Joe Stowell on Christian Living*, www.ChristianBibleStudies.com,
2007, 32.

Chapter 16

1. Anne Graham Lotz, "The Solution to Sin," Daily Devotional for
February 17, AnGel Ministries, http://www.annegrahamlotz.com/resources/
daily-devotional/2/17.

2. Adam Clarke, *A Commentary and Critical Notes* (New York: Abingdon-
Cokesbury Press, 1826), WORD*search* CROSS e-book, under: "Jeremiah 33:6."

Chapter 17

1. *The Preacher's Outline & Sermon Bible—Isaiah 2* (Chattanooga, TN: Leadership
Ministries Worldwide, 2005), WORD*search* CROSS e-book, under: "A. Set Free
Through God's Salvation and Greatness, 40:1–31."

2. James Strong, *Strong's Talking Greek & Hebrew Dictionary* (Austin, TX:
WORD*search* Corp., 2007), WORD*search* CROSS e-book, under: "1319."

About the Author

Julie-Allyson Ieron is a perceptive journalist who investigates God's truth and crafts her discoveries in ways that engage your mind and resonate with your heart. Her passion is to open God's Word alongside you to equip you to apply its riches to your daily joys, questions, and challenges.

Julie recently celebrated twenty-five years as an author, writing coach, editor, and conference speaker. Her ministry-defining project was released in 2010: *The Julie-Allyson Ieron Bible Reference Collection* on WORD*search* 9.0. It features nine of Julie's books linked with seventy-five Bible reference resources. Additionally, many of her books are available in MP3 audio and e-book formats, as well as print. *The Overwhelmed Woman's Guide to . . . Caring for Aging Parents* is a featured resource for *Focus on the Family*, where she was a radio guest.

Julie's personal life is as dynamic as her writing. She is her dad's medical advocate and along with her mom, Joy, daily administers his tests, meds, and shots.

In more relaxed times, Julie and Joy play violin and organ duets for weddings and church services (sometimes for funerals, too). Julie plays violin in her church's orchestra and regional hymn singing ensemble, dabbles in art for fun, and plays a killer game of Scrabble™.

Visit her online at http://theGODinterviews.blogspot.com.

If we may assist you in knowing more about Christ and the Christian life, please write us without obligation:

Joy Media, PO Box 1099, Park Ridge, IL 60068

or leave us a note at http://theGODinterviews.blogspot.com.